365 LESSONS FROM THE
STOICS

COMPILED BY ANDREA KIRK ASSAF

William Collins
an imprint of HarperCollins*Publishers*
1 London Bridge Street
London SE1 9GF

WilliamCollinsBooks.com

HarperCollins*Publishers*
Macken House, 39/40 Mayor Street Upper,
Dublin 1, D01 C9W8, Ireland

First published by HarperCollins*Publishers* in 2024
This William Collins paperback edition published in 2026

1 3 5 7 9 10 8 6 4 2

Copyright © HarperCollinsPublishers 2026

Compiled by Andrea Kirk Assaf
Cover and interior page design by e-Digital Design Ltd
Senior editor: Simon Holland

Andrea Kirk Assaf asserts the moral right to be identified
as the compiler of this work.

A catalogue record for this book is available from the British Library.

ISBN: 978-0-00-872968-4

Printed and bound in the UK using 100% renewable electricity
at CPI Group (UK) Ltd.

All rights reserved. No part of this publication may be reproduced,
stored in a retrieval system or transmitted, in any form or by any means,
electronic, mechanical, photocopying, recording or otherwise,
without the prior permission of the publishers.

Without limiting the exclusive rights of any author, contributor or the publisher of
this publication, any unauthorised use of this publication to train generative artificial
intelligence (AI) technologies is expressly prohibited. HarperCollins also exercise
their rights under Article 4(3) of the Digital Single Market Directive 2019/790 and
expressly reserve this publication from the text and data mining exception.

This book is sold subject to the condition that it shall not, by way of trade
or otherwise, be lent, re-sold, hired out or otherwise circulated without
the publisher's prior consent in any form of binding or cover other than that
in which it is published and without a similar condition including this
condition being imposed on the subsequent purchaser.

This book is produced from independently certified FSC™ paper
to ensure responsible forest management.

For more information visit: www.harpercollins.co.uk/green

365 LESSONS FROM THE
STOICS

Transform your Daily Life

Using the Stoics' Wisdom

and Understanding

FEATURING QUOTES FROM SENECA, EPICTETUS AND MARCUS AURELIUS

COMPILED BY ANDREA KIRK ASSAF

WILLIAM COLLINS

I dedicate this book to the memory of my father,
Russell Amos Kirk, who introduced me to Stoicism
through both word and example.

He kept his Stoic principles close throughout his life,
tempered by Christian hope.

CONTENTS

How to use this book	6
Introduction to the Stoics and Stoicism	9
365 Lessons	15
Index by theme	250
Index by Stoic	252
Further reading	254
Acknowledgements	255

HOW TO USE THIS BOOK

What would a Stoic's day look like? And how could this small, portable book of Stoic quotes be a useful companion through it? A Stoic's day is marked by mindfulness, discipline and reflection. This collection of Stoic quotes aims to be your companion through it all. With this volume on the nightstand, you can start your day by recalling the words of Marcus Aurelius, perhaps the most famous of all Stoics. He wrote this dialogue with himself while residing in a military camp by the Danube river.

"In the morning when thou risest unwillingly, let this thought be present – I am rising to the work of a human being. Why then am I dissatisfied if I am going to do the things for which I exist and for which I was brought into the world? Or have I been made for this, to lie in the bed-clothes and keep myself warm? But this is more pleasant. Dost thou exist then to take thy pleasure, and not at all for action or exertion? Dost thou not see the little plants, the little birds, the ants, the spiders, the bees working together to put in order their several parts of the universe? And art thou unwilling to do the work of a human being, and dost thou not make haste to do that which is according to thy nature?"

Once the feet have touched the ground and the challenge of life has been accepted, it is the ideal time to make a statement of affirmation and gratitude. In Aurelius' words: *"When you arise in the morning, think of what a precious privilege it is to be alive – to breathe, to think, to enjoy, to love."*

As the Stoic embarks upon the day, fraught with opportunities to grow in virtue through exercising one's 'ruling principle', it might help every now and then to take this book out of the bag or the desk drawer, to give oneself a reality check in order to mentally prepare for the worst-case scenario. Or, as our philosopher-king put it:

"…tell yourself: the people I deal with today will be meddling, ungrateful, arrogant, dishonest, jealous and surly. They are like this because they can't tell good from evil. But I have seen the beauty of good, and the ugliness of evil, and have recognized that the wrongdoer has a nature related to my own – not of the same blood and birth, but the same mind, and possessing a share of the divine. And so none of them can hurt me. No one can implicate me in ugliness. Nor can I feel angry at my relative, or hate him. We were born to work together like feet, hands and eyes, like the two rows of teeth, upper and lower. To obstruct each other is unnatural. To feel anger at someone, to turn your back on him: these are unnatural."

At nightfall, one can again imitate the example of Marcus, who nightly withdrew into his own mind and reflected upon all that had transpired, often through writing in his diary. Placing a journal next to this book, or even scribbling in the book itself, would encourage the adoption of another crucial Stoic habit – an end-of-the-day personal review through journalling.

As the eyelids close, one can retain these beautiful and heartening words of Seneca:

"…as we go to sleep, let us, in a pleasant and cheerful temper, say, I've lived. If God is pleased to add to our days the morrow, let us accept it with thanksgiving. Whoever hath said overnight I have lived, rises the next morn to gain."

Memento Mori, remember your death, is perhaps the most well known of the Stoic sayings, and this nightly reflection reminds us that each day is a life unto itself and that tomorrow is not guaranteed. As Seneca says: *"…every day is another step in life."*

Supporting your day with these Stoic sayings, as bookends from dawn to dark, may you find this little book to be a trusted companion on your own life journey.

INTRODUCTION TO THE STOICS AND STOICISM

Wisdom. Courage. Justice. Temperance. These are what are known as the four Stoic virtues that students of the philosophy strive to cultivate through reading, reasoning, dialogue and habitual practices. The value of these virtues, one could argue, is that they all assist in the attainment of another very practical virtue that is in great demand today – resilience.

The Stoics were realists who taught that most circumstances in life are beyond our control, a truth many of the younger generations have been confronted with since the Covid-19 lockdown deprived them of many personal freedoms they had taken for granted. Unlike the 'greatest generation', who were taught resilience through the harrowing experiences and hardships of World War II, the generations since have lived – at least in the Western world – in relative security. And so, when disaster strikes and foundations are shaken, as inevitably occurs, the perennial wisdom of the Stoics resurfaces and is given fresh relevance.

We are in a moment such as this. You may find, as you dip into these pages, that the three voices in this book, though their bones turned to dust two millennia ago, sound as if they are speaking directly to your daily struggles. This is no accident, for each author confronted the same realities of human nature that we do today – from resisting the temptation to stay in a warm, comfortable bed in the morning, to tempering anger in the face of injustices or disappointments throughout the day, to night-time sleepless enslavement to fears and anxieties regarding the future.

These things said, Stoicism provides more than wise words to turn to in times of crisis. It offers a deeply formative method for character development through practices that modern-day readers will be familiar with – mindfulness, gratitude, intentionality, affirmation, introspection, habit-building, emotional regulation and magnanimity. The Stoic is not born equipped with these superpowers; such capabilities are cultivated through trial and error, one moment at a time, fostering resilience.

"When force of circumstance upsets your equanimity, lose no time in recovering your self-control, and do not remain out of tune longer than you can help. Habitual recurrence to the harmony will increase your mastery of it." – Marcus Aurelius

Stoicism is a philosophy of action, not just theory. It exists, as all philosophies do, for the purpose of providing reasoned principles to serve as guides in the formation of mindset, moral action and *eudaimonia* – translated as 'human flourishing', or 'a well-lived life'. The three thinkers presented here are representative of Stoic philosophy in general, which accounts for their name recognition, and the three works selected are, in turn, representative of their thought. Allow me to present them to you in the context of their Stoic lineage.

It all began with a storm at sea in the third century BCE. A successful merchant of the highly prized Tyrian dye lost his ship and his entire fortune with it, washing ashore penniless in Greece. Zeno of Citium, as he was known, turned to the consolation of philosophy in Athens – first studying under Crates of Thebes, the founder of the Cynic school, before founding his own school. Zeno's students gathered on a painted porch in the Agora – the *stoa poikilê* – and came to be called Stoics.

Each of Zeno's successors left his own mark on Stoicism – Cleanthes, Chrysippus, Zeno of Tarsus, Diogenes of Babylon, Antipater of Tarsus and Panaetius of Rhodes. Stoicism spread to Rome and was championed by such diverse individuals as Roman statesmen Cato the Younger and Seneca the Younger, the freed Greek slave Epictetus (as recorded by his student Arrian), and, most famously, the emperor of the Roman empire himself, Marcus Aurelius.

With the fall of the Roman Empire, over two hundred years would pass before Stoicism was rediscovered and appreciated by great Christian minds such as St. Ambrose, St. Augustine, St. Jerome and Boethius. Stoicism's next dusting-off and repolishing came about thanks to the Flemish Renaissance humanist Justus Lipsius, who led a philosophical movement in the late sixteenth century that combined Stoic virtues with Christian beliefs. Lipsius promoted Stoicism in part as a response to the religious wars of the day, and it was during this time that Stoicism was referred to as a 'crisis philosophy', with Lipsius advocating the virtue of 'constancy' in the face of political and religious upheaval.

Although Stoic physics and logic were largely abandoned, their virtue ethics continued to shape philosophy and theology – notably in the work of René Descartes, Benedict de Spinoza and Blaise Pascal – up to today. In the twentieth century, with the development of rational emotive behaviour therapy by Albert Ellis, and then cognitive behavioural therapy by Aaron T. Beck, Stoicism found a partner in modern scientific inquiry and application. The twenty-first century has seen such a resurgence of interest in the philosophy, particularly in the last few years since the pandemic, that it has been given a new name – Modern Stoicism – with a focus on harnessing the ability of Stoic principles and practices for the prevention of potential mental health issues surrounding trauma and stress.

Returning to the three Stoic authors of ancient Rome featured in these pages, let us understand the complex realities each one lived through, which led them to write these words that we can now read today for our own benefit.

Lucius Annaeus Seneca, also known as Seneca the Younger, was a Roman statesman, orator, playwright – and, of course, Stoic philosopher. Living between 4 BCE and 65 CE, Seneca had the misfortune to be a leading intellectual figure during the reign of emperors Caligula, who nearly killed him, Claudius, who sent him into exile, and then Nero, who ordered him to commit suicide. In between these tragedies, Seneca was a powerful quaestor, private tutor to the future emperor Nero, and de facto co-ruler of Rome during the early years of Nero's reign. Withdrawing from political intrigue in his final years of retirement, he authored the majority of his Stoic work, including the 124 letters to his younger friend Lucilius, full of personal anecdotes, observations and advice, particularly about the beauty and wisdom of cooperating with nature.

Epictetus lived in Rome during the last decades of Seneca's life and would certainly be aware of the famous statesman's career, writings and demise, though Epictetus was in a very different social class. Born as a Greek slave in Phrygia, Epictetus lived most of his life in Rome as the property of Nero's secretary, Epaphroditus. A gifted intellect, Epictetus was sent to study under the Stoic philosopher Musonius Rufus. Following the death of Nero and then his master, Epictetus obtained his freedom and began teaching philosophy in Rome, only to be banished by the emperor Domitian in 93 CE, along with all philosophers. The remaining years of his long life were spent teaching at a school he founded in Greece, where his pupil Arrian recorded his wisdom in *The Discourses and The Enchiridion*, or Handbook. He urged his students, in his sarcastic and reprimanding style, to recall that Stoicism is a way of life – *modus vivendi* – not mere theory. External events are beyond our control, Epictetus explains, but we can control our reactions to them, through consistent self-discipline.

Marcus Aurelius is history's most unlikely example of a Stoic. From childhood he demonstrated a virtuous character, and even during his lifetime he was known as the philosopher-king, that rare combination of a man of both contemplation and action. Marcus Aurelius Antoninus became heir to the Nerva-Antonine dynasty through adoption and was groomed to rule. He was also educated for wisdom and was well read in the Stoic tradition, including the works of Epictetus. Our modern concept of Stoicism largely comes from Marcus' private writings, never intended for publication, but nevertheless widely read ever since its public appearance in 180 CE. In *Meditations* we encounter a figure who continually took recourse to the consolation of philosophy as he faced one war after another, a plague of historic proportions, and the deaths of seven of his children. Marcus' continual reminder to himself was about the brevity of life, and the rewards of living it virtuously. Or, as he so succinctly puts it: *"Do not act as if thou wert going to live ten thousand years. Death hangs over thee. While thou livest, while it is in thy power, be good."*

Finally, let's conclude by again heeding the exhortation of this resilient philosopher-king, who spent approximately nineteen years giving himself the following advice in his diary: *"No longer talk at all about the kind of man that a good man ought to be, but be such."*

Andrea Kirk Assaf
May, 2024
Rome, Italy

365 LESSONS

VIRTUE

God has not only given us these faculties, by which we shall be able to bear everything that happens without being depressed or broken by it; but, like a good king and a true father, He has given us these faculties free from hindrance, subject to no compulsion, unimpeded, and has put them entirely in our own power, without even having reserved to Himself any power of hindering or impeding. You, who have received these powers free and as your own, use them not; you do not even see what you have received, and from whom; some of you being blinded to the giver, and not even acknowledging your benefactor, and others, through meanness of spirit, betaking yourselves to fault-finding and making charges against God. Yet I will show to you that you have powers and means for greatness of soul and manliness; but what powers you have for finding fault and making accusations, do you show me.

EPICTETUS, *THE TEACHINGS OF A STOIC: SELECTED DISCOURSES AND THE ENCHIRIDION,* "OF PROVIDENCE" (FROM C. EARLY 2ND CENTURY CE)

ACCEPTANCE

Every moment think steadily as a Roman and a man to do what thou hast in hand with perfect and simple dignity, and feeling of affection, and freedom, and justice; and to give thyself relief from all other thoughts. And thou wilt give thyself relief, if thou doest every act of thy life as if it were the last, laying aside all carelessness and passionate aversion from the commands of reason, and all hypocrisy, and self-love, and discontent with the portion which has been given to thee.

MARCUS AURELIUS, *MEDITATIONS*, "BOOK II" (FROM C. 180 CE)

VIRTUE

We likewise may overcome everything if we would consider that the reward proposed to us is not a simple coronet, a palm, or the trumpet commanding silence at the proclamation of our honour, but virtue, strength of mind and everlasting peace, if in any conflict we have subdued fortune.

LUCIUS SENECA, *LETTERS FROM A STOIC*, "LXXVIII. ON SICKNESS, PAIN AND DEATH" (FROM C. 63-65 CE)

TIME

Do not act as if thou wert going to live ten thousand years. Death hangs over thee. While thou livest, while it is in thy power, be good.

MARCUS AURELIUS, *MEDITATIONS*, "BOOK IV" (FROM C. 180 CE)

DETACHMENT

Remember that desire contains in it the profession (hope) of obtaining that which you desire; and the profession (hope) in aversion (turning from a thing) is that you will not fall into that which you attempt to avoid; and he who fails in his desire is unfortunate; and he who falls into that which he would avoid is unhappy. If then you attempt to avoid only the things contrary to nature which are within your power you will not be involved in any of the things which you would avoid. But if you attempt to avoid disease, or death, or poverty, you will be unhappy. Take away then aversion from all things which are not in our power, and transfer it to the things contrary to nature which are in our power.

EPICTETUS, *THE TEACHINGS OF A STOIC: SELECTED DISCOURSES AND THE ENCHIRIDION*, "THE MANUAL: II" (FROM C. EARLY 2ND CENTURY CE)

DETACHMENT

Where is the nature of evil and good? It is where truth is: where truth is and where nature is, there is caution: where truth is, there is courage where nature is. For this reason also it is ridiculous to say, Suggest something to me (tell me what to do). What should I suggest to you? Well, form my mind so as to accommodate itself to any event. Why that is just the same as if a man who is ignorant of letters should say, Tell me what to write when any name is proposed to me... But if you have practised writing, you are also prepared to write (or to do) anything that is required. If you are not, what can I now suggest? For if circumstances require something else, what will you say, or what will you do? Remember then this general precept and you will need no suggestion. But if you gape after externals, you must of necessity ramble up and down in obedience to the will of your master. And who is the master? He who has the power over the things which you seek to gain or try to avoid.

EPICTETUS, *THE TEACHINGS OF A STOIC:
SELECTED DISCOURSES AND THE ENCHIRIDION*,
"OF TRANQUILITY (FREEDOM FROM PERTURBATION)"
(FROM C. EARLY 2ND CENTURY CE)

GOODNESS

The maker, says he, is God, from what it is made matter...
He is good and all that he hath made is good, and being
good he cannot envy any good to his creatures and therefore
he hath made the world in its best fashion and furnished it in
the best manner possible.

**LUCIUS SENECA, *LETTERS FROM A STOIC*, "LXV. ON THE
FIRST CAUSE" (FROM C. 63-65 CE)**

WISDOM

I shall keep watching myself continually, and – a most useful
habit – shall review each day. For this is what makes us
wicked: that no one of us looks back over his own life. Our
thoughts are devoted only to what we are about to do. And
yet our plans for the future always depend on the past.

**LUCIUS SENECA, *LETTERS FROM A STOIC*, "LXXVIII. ON
SICKNESS, PAIN AND DEATH" (FROM C. 63-65 CE)**

COOPERATION WITH NATURE

Begin the morning by saying to thyself, I shall meet with the busybody, the ungrateful, arrogant, deceitful, envious, unsocial. All these things happen to them by reason of their ignorance of what is good and evil. But I who have seen the nature of the good that it is beautiful, and of the bad that it is ugly, and the nature of him who does wrong, that it is akin to me, not only of the same blood or seed, but that it participates in the same intelligence and the same portion of the divinity, I can neither be injured by any of them, for no one can fix on me what is ugly, nor can I be angry with my kinsman, nor hate him. For we are made for cooperation, like feet, like hands, like eyelids, like the rows of the upper and lower teeth. To act against one another then is contrary to nature; and it is acting against one another to be vexed and to turn away.

MARCUS AURELIUS, *MEDITATIONS*, "BOOK II" (FROM C. 180 CE)

VIRTUE

The best way of avenging thyself is not to become like the wrongdoer.

MARCUS AURELIUS, *MEDITATIONS*, "BOOK VI" (FROM C. 180 CE)

VIRTUE

He who is making progress, having learned from philosophers that desire means the desire of good things, and aversion means aversion from bad things; having learned too that happiness and tranquillity are not attainable by man otherwise than by not failing to obtain what he desires, and not falling into that which he would avoid; such a man takes from himself desire altogether and confers it, but he employs his aversion only on things which are dependent on his will. For if he attempts to avoid anything independent of his will, he knows that sometimes he will fall in with something which he wishes to avoid, and he will be unhappy. Now if virtue promises good fortune and tranquillity and happiness, certainly also the progress towards virtue is progress towards each of these things. For it is always true that to whatever point the perfecting of anything leads us, progress is an approach towards this point.

EPICTETUS, *THE TEACHINGS OF A STOIC: SELECTED DISCOURSES AND THE ENCHIRIDION*, "OF PROGRESS OR IMPROVEMENT" (FROM C. EARLY 2ND CENTURY CE)

VIRTUE

Consider with yourself for some time whether such a one is worthy to be received into your bosom, and if he seems a proper person, admit him with your whole heart. Converse as frankly and boldly with him as you would with your own self. Yet live so, Lucilius, as to commit nothing but what you dare trust even with an enemy. However, as many things may intervene, which, from their own nature or custom are termed secrets, these belong to the province of a friend with whom you must communicate all your cares and all your counsels.

LUCIUS SENECA, *LETTERS FROM A STOIC*, "III. ON FRIENDSHIP" (FROM C. 63-65 CE)

WISDOM

Philosophy does not propose to secure for a man any external thing. If it did (or if it were not, as I say), philosophy would be allowing some thing which is not within its province. For as the carpenter's material is wood, and that of the statuary is copper, so the matter of the art of living is each man's life.

EPICTETUS, *THE TEACHINGS OF A STOIC: SELECTED DISCOURSES AND THE ENCHIRIDION*, "WHAT PHILOSOPHY PROMISES" (FROM C. EARLY 2ND CENTURY CE)

GOODNESS

From everything, which is or happens in the world, it is easy to praise Providence, if a man possesses these two qualities: the faculty of seeing what belongs and happens to all persons and things, and a grateful disposition. If he does not possess these two qualities, one man will not see the use of things which are and which happen: another will not be thankful for them, even if he does know them.

EPICTETUS, *THE TEACHINGS OF A STOIC: SELECTED DISCOURSES AND THE ENCHIRIDION*, "OF PROVIDENCE" (FROM C. EARLY 2ND CENTURY CE)

COOPERATION WITH NATURE

The food profits not, nor gives due nourishment to the body that abides not some time therein. Nothing so much prevents the recovery of health as a frequent change of supposed remedies. A wound is not soon healed when different salves are tried by way of experiment. A plant thrives not, nor can well take root, that is moved from place to place. What profits only accidentally, in passing, is of little use.

LUCIUS SENECA, *LETTERS FROM A STOIC*, "II. ON STUDY, AND TRUE RICHES" (FROM C. 63-65 CE)

WISDOM

As we go to sleep, let us, in a pleasant and cheerful temper, say, I've lived, I've run the defined course of fate. If God is pleased to add to our days the morrow, let us accept it with thanksgiving. He is a most happy man and truly enjoys himself who expects the morrow without the least anxiety, whoever hath said overnight I have lived, rises the next morn to gain.

LUCIUS SENECA, *LETTERS FROM A STOIC*, "XII. ON LIFE AND OLD AGE" (FROM C. 63-65 CE)

ACCEPTANCE

Be like the promontory against which the waves continually break, but it stands firm and tames the fury of the water around it. Unhappy am I because this has happened to me? Not so, but happy am I, though this has happened to me, because I continue free from pain, neither crushed by the present nor fearing the future. For such a thing as this might have happened to every man; but every man would not have continued free from pain on such an occasion.

MARCUS AURELIUS, *MEDITATIONS*, "BOOK IV" (FROM C. 180 CE)

ACCEPTANCE

If you would have your children and your wife and your friends to live forever, you are silly; for you would have the things which are not in your power to be in your power, and the things which belong to others to be yours… He is the master of every man who has the power over the things which another person wishes or does not wish, the power to confer them on him or to take them away. Whoever then wishes to be free let him neither wish for anything nor avoid anything which depends on others: if he does not observe this rule, he must be a slave.

EPICTETUS, *THE TEACHINGS OF A STOIC: SELECTED DISCOURSES AND THE ENCHIRIDION*, "THE MANUAL: XIV" (FROM C. EARLY 2ND CENTURY CE)

DETACHMENT

I can have that opinion about anything, which I ought to have. If I can, why am I disturbed? The things which are external to my mind have no relation at all to my mind. Let this be the state of thy affects, and thou standest erect. To recover thy life is in thy power. Look at things again as thou didst use to look at them; for in this consists the recovery of thy life.

MARCUS AURELIUS, *MEDITATIONS*, "BOOK VII" (FROM C. 180 CE)

NOBILITY OF THOUGHT

It demands my approbation and gives me infinite pleasure to find, Lucilius, that you pursue your studies with attention and make it the chief to improve daily in goodness and virtue. I not only exhort but earnestly beseech you to persevere. But this too I must advise you, that you affect not to be singular, either in your dress or manner of life, like those who are ambitious not with a design of doing any good but of being taken notice of. Pretend not to an uncouth habit, slovenly to neglect the hair and beard, to declare a sworn aversion to a piece of plate, to lie on the ground, or to exhibit any other extraordinary mark of perverse ambition… Let us act upon this principle not to lead a life contrary to the generality of men but a better one, otherwise they whom we propose to instruct and reform will fly from and avoid us.

LUCIUS SENECA, *LETTERS FROM A STOIC*, "V. AGAINST THE AFFECTATION OF SINGULARITY – ON HOPE AND FEAR" (FROM C. 63–65 CE)

WISDOM

The wise and good man then, after considering all these things, submits his own mind to him who administers the whole, as good citizens do to the law of the state. He who is receiving instruction ought to come to be instructed with this intention. How shall I follow the gods in all things, how shall I be contented with the divine administration, and how can I become free? For he is free to whom everything happens according to his will, and whom no man can hinder. What then, is freedom madness? Certainly not; for madness and freedom do not consist. But, you say, I would have everything result just as I like, and in whatever way I like. You are mad, you are beside yourself. Do you not know that freedom is a noble and valuable thing? But for me inconsiderately to wish for things to happen as I inconsiderately like, this appears to be not only not noble, but even most base.

EPICTETUS, *THE TEACHINGS OF A STOIC:*
SELECTED DISCOURSES AND THE ENCHIRIDION, "OF
CONTENTMENT" (FROM C. EARLY 2ND CENTURY CE)

COOPERATION WITH NATURE

For to delight in bustle and tumult is not industry, but the conflict of a disordered mind, nor is it to be called ease, that thinks even the least motion irksome, but rather languor and dissipation. I will therefore recommend to you what I read in Pomponius. There have been those, says he, who have so devoted themselves to solitude, in some dark corner, as to think everything without to be trouble and confusion. These two things are to be interwoven, as it were, together: Rest and Labour. If you examine Nature she will tell you that she made both the Day and the Night.

LUCIUS SENECA, *LETTERS FROM A STOIC*, "III. ON FRIENDSHIP" (FROM C. 63-65 CE)

WILL

Nature hath given us feet to walk withal, as well as eyes to see with for ourselves. I know that an indulgence of this kind is apt to weaken one and we may leave off walking until by disuse we cannot walk at all…

LUCIUS SENECA, *LETTERS FROM A STOIC*, "LV. A TRUE FRIEND IS NEVER ABSENT" (FROM C. 63-65 CE)

WILL

24

Do the things external which fall upon thee distract thee? Give thyself time to learn something new and good, and cease to be whirled around. But then thou must also avoid being carried about the other way. For those too are triflers who have wearied themselves in life by their activity, and yet have no object to which to direct every movement, and, in a word, all their thoughts.

MARCUS AURELIUS, *MEDITATIONS*, "BOOK II" (FROM C. 180 CE)

WISDOM

25

…you will say you have a mind sometimes to amuse yourself with one book and sometimes with another. It is a sign, my friend, of a nice and squeamish stomach to be tasting many viands, which, as they are various and of different qualities, rather corrupt than nourish. Read, therefore, always the most approved authors, and if you are pleased at any time to taste others by way of amusement, still return to those as your principal study.

LUCIUS SENECA, *LETTERS FROM A STOIC*, "II. ON STUDY, AND TRUE RICHES" (FROM C. 63-65 CE)

COOPERATION WITH NATURE

Thou must now at last perceive of what universe thou art a part, and of what administrator of the universe thy existence is an efflux, and that a limit of time is fixed for thee, which if thou dost not use for clearing away the clouds from thy mind, it will go and thou wilt go, and it will never return.

MARCUS AURELIUS, *MEDITATIONS*, "BOOK II" (FROM C. 180 CE)

WISDOM

…no one can live happily, or indeed scarce tolerably, without the study of philosophy, and that wisdom when perfected makes life completely happy and, without having made any great progress, satisfactory. But this opinion, clear as it is, must be established and fixed deeper in the heart by daily meditation. It is more difficult to abide by good resolutions than to form them. You must persevere and by continual application so strengthen the mind that it may be as truly good as the will is to have it so.

LUCIUS SENECA, *LETTERS FROM A STOIC*, "XVI. ON THE STUDY OF PHILOSOPHY" (FROM C. 63-65 CE)

COOPERATION WITH NATURE

Through not observing what is in the mind of another a man has seldom been seen to be unhappy; but those who do not observe the movements of their own minds must of necessity be unhappy. This thou must always bear in mind, what is the nature of the whole, and what is my nature, and how this is related to that, and what kind of a part it is of what kind of a whole; and that there is no one who hinders thee from always doing and saying the things which are according to the nature of which thou art a part.

MARCUS AURELIUS, *MEDITATIONS*, "BOOK II" (FROM C. 180 CE)

NOBILITY OF THOUGHT

Be continually treasuring something to arm you against poverty, something against the fear of death and other like evils incident to man. And when you have read sufficiently, make a reserve of some particular sentiment for that day's meditation. Such is my own practice, of the many things I read I generally select one for observation.

LUCIUS SENECA, *LETTERS FROM A STOIC*,
"II. ON STUDY, AND TRUE RICHES" (FROM C. 63-65 CE)

WISDOM

Now this is what philosophy chiefly recommends to her pupils: sound sense, common humanity and the social virtues, so as to converse with those whom the disparity of our profession separates us from. Let us also beware, left intending to be admired, that we make ourselves ridiculous and odious. Our business is to live according to Nature, but it is contrary to Nature to afflict the body, to hate decency and cleanliness and to diet one's self, not only with cheap food but with such as is gross and horrid. As it is luxury to covet dainties, it is folly and madness to reject such things as are in common use and easily to be obtained. Philosophy preaches temperance and frugality, not severe mortification, and frugality may be decent and not inelegant. This, then, is the mean that I should choose, a life tempered between politeness and vulgarity; let all men admire it, but at the same time see and acknowledge that there is nothing so extraordinary in it but what is practicable.

LUCIUS SENECA, *LETTERS FROM A STOIC*, "V. AGAINST THE AFFECTATION OF SINGULARITY – ON HOPE AND FEAR" (FROM C. 63-65 CE)

WISDOM

31

What a man applies himself to earnestly, that he naturally loves. Do men then apply themselves earnestly to the things which are bad? By no means. Well, do they apply themselves to things which in no way concern themselves? Not to these either. It remains then that they employ themselves earnestly only about things which are good; and if they are earnestly employed about things, they love such things also. Whoever then understands what is good can also know how to love; but he who cannot distinguish good from bad, and things which are neither good nor bad from both, how can he possess the power of loving? To love, then, is only in the power of the wise.

**EPICTETUS, *THE TEACHINGS OF A STOIC:
SELECTED DISCOURSES AND THE ENCHIRIDION*,
"ON FRIENDSHIP" (FROM C. EARLY 2ND CENTURY CE)**

VIRTUE

32

And if you ever wish to exercise yourself in labour and endurance, do it for yourself, and not for others.

**EPICTETUS, *THE TEACHINGS OF A STOIC: SELECTED
DISCOURSES AND THE ENCHIRIDION*, "THE MANUAL: XLVII"
(FROM C. EARLY 2ND CENTURY CE)**

WILL

Where is the good? In the will. Where is the evil? In the will. Where is neither of them? In those things which are independent of the will.

EPICTETUS, *THE TEACHINGS OF A STOIC: SELECTED DISCOURSES AND THE ENCHIRIDION*, "THAT WE DO NOT STRIVE TO USE OUR OPINIONS ABOUT GOOD AND EVIL" (FROM C. EARLY 2ND CENTURY CE)

ACCEPTANCE

But not one of us chooses, even when necessity summons, readily to obey it, but weeping and groaning we suffer what we do suffer, and we call them "circumstances". What kind of circumstances, man? If you give the name of circumstances to the things which are around you, all things are circumstances; but if you call hardships by this name, what hardship is there in the dying of that which has been produced? But that which destroys is either a sword, or a wheel, or the sea, or a tile, or a tyrant. Why do you care about the way of going down to Hades? All ways are equal.

EPICTETUS, *THE TEACHINGS OF A STOIC: SELECTED DISCOURSES AND THE ENCHIRIDION*, "OF INDIFFERENCE" (FROM C. EARLY 2ND CENTURY CE)

DETACHMENT

...a man only loses that which he has. I have lost my garment. The reason is that you had a garment. I have a pain in my head. Have you any pain in your horns? Why then are you troubled? For we only lose those things, we have only pains about those things, which we possess.

EPICTETUS, *THE TEACHINGS OF A STOIC: SELECTED DISCOURSES AND THE ENCHIRIDION,* "THAT WE OUGHT NOT TO BE ANGRY WITH THE ERRORS (FAULTS) OF OTHERS" (FROM C. EARLY 2ND CENTURY CE)

TIME

Though thou shouldst be going to live three thousand years, and as many times ten thousand years, still remember that no man loses any other life than this which he now lives, nor lives any other than this which he now loses. The longest and shortest are thus brought to the same. For the present is the same to all, though that which perishes is not the same; and so that which is lost appears to be a mere moment. For a man cannot lose either the past or the future: for what a man has not, how can anyone take this from him?

MARCUS AURELIUS, *MEDITATIONS,* "BOOK II" (FROM C. 180 CE)

TIME

Brute beasts fly such dangers as they are sensible of and, having escaped them, rest secure. But we are tortured, both with what is past and what is to come. Thus many things, really good in themselves, hurt us, for memory recalls and forecast anticipates the torment of fear. No one is wretched from what is present only.

LUCIUS SENECA, *LETTERS FROM A STOIC*, "V. AGAINST THE AFFECTATION OF SINGULARITY – ON HOPE AND FEAR" (FROM C. 63-65 CE)

WILL

What then should a man have in readiness in such circumstances? What else than this? What is mine, and what is not mine; and what is permitted to me, and what is not permitted to me. I must die. Must I then die lamenting? I must be put in chains. Must I then also lament? I must go into exile. Does any man then hinder me from going with smiles and cheerfulness and contentment?

EPICTETUS, *THE TEACHINGS OF A STOIC: SELECTED DISCOURSES AND THE ENCHIRIDION*, "OF THE THINGS WHICH ARE IN OUR POWER AND NOT IN OUR POWER" (FROM C. EARLY 2ND CENTURY CE)

VIRTUE

Labour not unwillingly, nor without regard to the common interest, nor without due consideration, nor with distraction; nor let studied ornament set off thy thoughts, and be not either a man of many words, or busy about too many things… Be cheerful also, and seek not external help nor the tranquility which others give. A man then must stand erect, not be kept erect by others.

MARCUS AURELIUS, *MEDITATIONS*, "BOOK III"
(FROM C. 180 CE)

WISDOM

Some people are apt to blab to everyone they meet what ought to be entrusted only with friends, and to disburden themselves of whatever may chance to wring them, by teasing every ear with the doleful tale. There are others who are afraid of the consciousness of their dearest conversants. Nay… they would not trust their own consciences with them. They are both in the wrong, it is no less a fault to trust everyone than to trust no one.

LUCIUS SENECA, *LETTERS FROM A STOIC*, "III.
ON FRIENDSHIP" (FROM C. 63-65 CE)

CHANGE

Thou art a little soul bearing about a corpse, as Epictetus used to say. It is no evil for things to undergo change, and no good for things to subsist in consequence of change. Time is like a river made up of the events which happen, and a violent stream; for as soon as a thing has been seen, it is carried away, and another comes in its place, and this will be carried away too. Everything which happens is as familiar and well known as the rose in spring and the fruit in summer; for such is disease, and death, and calumny, and treachery, and whatever else delights fools or vexes them. In the series of things those which follow are always aptly fitted to those which have gone before; for this series is not like a mere enumeration of disjoined things, which has only a necessary sequence, but it is a rational connection: and as all existing things are arranged together harmoniously, so the things which come into existence exhibit no mere succession, but a certain wonderful relationship.

MARCUS AURELIUS, *MEDITATIONS*, "BOOK IV" (FROM C. 180 CE)

DETACHMENT

We admire some animals in that they can pass through fire without detriment. How much more admirable is this philosopher, who without loss or harm, made his way, through fire, sword and ruin! You see how much easier it is to conquer a whole nation than one man. The like noble sentiment and language holds the Stoic. He carries his all, undamaged, through a city on fire, for he is contented in himself and under this character rates his happiness.

LUCIUS SENECA, *LETTERS FROM A STOIC*, "IX. ON FRIENDSHIP, SELF-COMPLACENCY AND CONTENTMENT" (FROM C. 63-65 CE)

VIRTUE

A good understanding is not to be hired or purchased, and I really think was it put to sale there would be but few bidders, whereas a bad one is often purchased and paid dearly for.

LUCIUS SENECA, *LETTERS FROM A STOIC*, "XXVII. VIRTUE ONLY IS SECURE" (FROM C. 63-65 CE)

WILL

44

What then is education? Education is the learning how to adapt the natural præcognitions to the particular things conformably to nature; and then to distinguish that of things some are in our power, but others are not. In our power are will and all acts which depend on the will; things not in our power are the body, the parts of the body, possessions, parents, brothers, children, country, and, generally, all with whom we live in society. In what then should we place the good? To what kind of things shall we adapt it? To the things which are in our power? Is not health then a good thing, and soundness of limb, and life, and are not children and parents and country?

EPICTETUS, *THE TEACHINGS OF A STOIC: SELECTED DISCOURSES AND THE ENCHIRIDION*, "ON PRECOGNITIONS" (FROM C. EARLY 2ND CENTURY CE)

VIRTUE

45

Do not be carried along inconsiderately by the appearance of things, but give help to all according to thy ability and their fitness…

MARCUS AURELIUS, *MEDITATIONS*, "BOOK V" (FROM C. 180 CE)

VIRTUE

It is circumstances (difficulties) which show what men are. Therefore when a difficulty falls upon you, remember that God, like a trainer of wrestlers, has matched you with a rough young man. For what purpose? you may say. Why, that you may become an Olympic conqueror; but it is not accomplished without sweat. In my opinion no man has had a more profitable difficulty than you have had, if you choose to make use of it as an athlete would deal with a young antagonist.

EPICTETUS, *THE TEACHINGS OF A STOIC: SELECTED DISCOURSES AND THE ENCHIRIDION*, "HOW WE SHOULD STRUGGLE WITH CIRCUMSTANCES" (FROM C. EARLY 2ND CENTURY CE)

WISDOM

Because the gods have given the vine, or wheat, we sacrifice to them; but because they have produced in the human mind that fruit by which they designed to show us the truth which relates to happiness, shall we not thank God for this?

EPICTETUS, *THE TEACHINGS OF A STOIC: SELECTED DISCOURSES AND THE ENCHIRIDION*, "OF PROGRESS OR IMPROVEMENT" (FROM C. EARLY 2ND CENTURY CE)

VIRTUE

I say the same of luxury, which sometimes seems to give way but soon again revives, soliciting those who have professed frugality, and in the midst of parsimony pursues the pleasures it had not entirely condemned but only left for a time and pursues them now the more vehemently as the more secretly it can obtain its desires. For the more public all vices are, they are the less daring. Diseases, likewise, are more easily curable when they break out and show themselves what they are, and you may be assured that avarice, ambition and all the evils of the human heart are the most dangerous when they subside and are patched up by a pretended cure.

LUCIUS SENECA, *LETTERS FROM A STOIC*, "LVI. ON TRANQUILLITY" (FROM C. 63-65 CE)

TIME

Everything is only for a day, both that which remembers and that which is remembered.

MARCUS AURELIUS, *MEDITATIONS*, "BOOK IV" (FROM C. 180 CE)

DETACHMENT

Now that which does not make a man worse, how can it make a man's life worse? But neither through ignorance, nor having the knowledge, but not the power to guard against or correct these things, is it possible that the nature of the universe has overlooked them; nor is it possible that it has made so great a mistake, either through want of power or want of skill, that good and evil should happen indiscriminately to the good and the bad. But death certainly, and life, honour and dishonour, pain and pleasure, all these things equally happen to good men and bad, being things which make us neither better nor worse. Therefore they are neither good nor evil.

MARCUS AURELIUS, *MEDITATIONS*, "BOOK II" (FROM C. 180 CE)

VIRTUE

…nothing delights so much as the examples of the virtues, when they are exhibited in the morals of those who live with us and present themselves in abundance, as far as is possible. Wherefore we must keep them before us.

MARCUS AURELIUS, *MEDITATIONS*, "BOOK VI" (FROM C. 180 CE)

GOODNESS

All that is from the gods is full of Providence. That which is from fortune is not separated from nature or without an interweaving and involution with the things which are ordered by Providence. From thence all things flow; and there is besides necessity, and that which is for the advantage of the whole universe, of which thou art a part. But that is good for every part of nature which the nature of the whole brings, and what serves to maintain this nature. Now the universe is preserved, as by the changes of the elements so by the changes of things compounded of the elements. Let these principles be enough for thee, let them always be fixed opinions.

MARCUS AURELIUS, *MEDITATIONS*, "BOOK II" (FROM C. 180 CE)

ACCEPTANCE

Let death and exile and every other thing which appears dreadful be daily before your eyes; but most of all death: and you will never think of anything mean nor will you desire anything extravagantly.

EPICTETUS, *THE TEACHINGS OF A STOIC: SELECTED DISCOURSES AND THE ENCHIRIDION*, "THE MANUAL: XXI" (FROM C. EARLY 2ND CENTURY CE)

NOBILITY OF THOUGHT

You must attach yourself to some [authors] in particular and thoroughly digest what you read, if you would entrust the faithful memory with anything of use. He that is everywhere is nowhere. They who spend their time in travelling meet indeed with many a host but few friends. This is necessarily the case of those who apply not familiarly to any one study, but run over everything cursorily and in haste.

LUCIUS SENECA, *LETTERS FROM A STOIC*, "II. ON STUDY, AND TRUE RICHES" (FROM C. 63-65 CE)

NOBILITY OF THOUGHT

Nature hath formed us great and valiant. …so hath she given to man a glorious and lofty spirit that puts him upon searching where he may live most justly and decently, not where most safely, resembling the great world, which he follows, and emulates, as far as human ability will permit.

LUCIUS SENECA, *LETTERS FROM A STOIC*, "II. ON TRAVELLING" (FROM C. 63-65 CE)

COOPERATION WITH NATURE

If he is a stranger to the universe who does not know what is in it, no less is he a stranger who does not know what is going on in it. He is a runaway, who flies from social reason; he is blind, who shuts the eyes of the understanding; he is poor, who has need of another, and has not from himself all things which are useful for life. He is an abscess on the universe who withdraws and separates himself from the reason of our common nature through being displeased with the things which happen, for the same nature produces this, and has produced thee too: he is a piece rent asunder from the state, who tears his own soul from that of reasonable animals, which is one.

MARCUS AURELIUS, *MEDITATIONS*, "BOOK IV" (FROM C. 180 CE)

NOBILITY OF THOUGHT

If thou findest in human life anything better than justice, truth, temperance, fortitude, and, in a word, anything better than thy own mind's self-satisfaction in the things which it enables thee to do according to right reason, and in the condition that is assigned to thee without thy own choice; if, I say, thou seest anything better than this, turn to it with all thy soul, and enjoy that which thou hast found to be the best. But if nothing appears to be better than the deity which is planted in thee, which has subjected to itself all thy appetites, and carefully examines all the impressions, and, as Socrates said, has detached itself from the persuasions of sense, and has submitted itself to the gods, and cares for mankind; if thou findest everything else smaller and of less value than this, give place to nothing else, for if thou dost once diverge and incline to it, thou wilt no longer without distraction be able to give the preference to that good thing which is thy proper possession and thy own; for it is not right that anything of any other kind, such as praise from the many, or power, or enjoyment of pleasure, should come into competition with that which is rationally and politically or practically good.

MARCUS AURELIUS, *MEDITATIONS*, "BOOK III" (FROM C. 180 CE)

TIME

We ought to consider not only that our life is daily wasting away and a smaller part of it is left, but another thing also must be taken into the account, that if a man should live longer, it is quite uncertain whether the understanding will still continue sufficient for the comprehension of things, and retain the power of contemplation which strives to acquire the knowledge of the divine and the human… We must make haste then, not only because we are daily nearer to death, but also because the conception of things and the understanding of them cease first.

MARCUS AURELIUS, *MEDITATIONS*, "BOOK III" (FROM C. 180 CE)

WILL

Disease is an impediment to the body, but not to the will, unless the will itself chooses. Lameness is an impediment to the leg, but not to the will. And add this reflection on the occasion of everything that happens; for you will find it an impediment to something else, but not to yourself.

EPICTETUS, *THE TEACHINGS OF A STOIC: SELECTED DISCOURSES AND THE ENCHIRIDION*, "THE MANUAL: IX" (FROM C. EARLY 2ND CENTURY CE)

COOPERATION WITH NATURE

It is therefore enough for [animals] to eat and to drink, and to copulate, and to do all the other things which they severally do. But for us, to whom he has given also the intellectual faculty, these things are not sufficient; for unless we act in a proper and orderly manner, and conformably to the nature and constitution of each thing, we shall never attain our true end. For where the constitutions of living beings are different, there also the acts and the ends are different. In those animals then whose constitution is adapted only to use, use alone is enough; but in an animal (man), which has also the power of understanding the use, unless there be the due exercise of the understanding, he will never attain his proper end.

EPICTETUS, *THE TEACHINGS OF A STOIC: SELECTED DISCOURSES AND THE ENCHIRIDION*, "OF PROVIDENCE" (FROM C. EARLY 2ND CENTURY CE)

VIRTUE

Why is not a man ready to acknowledge his faults? Because he is as yet plunged in them. To tell a dream is the part of one awake, and to confess our imperfections is a token of sanity. Let us awake, therefore, that we may be sensible of and correct our errors. Now it is philosophy alone that will rouse us, 'tis she alone that will shake off a sound sleep. Dedicate yourself entirely to her, you are worthy of her and she of you. Embrace her most cordially, deny yourself to all besides, boldly, publicly. There is no reason that a philosopher should be at the will and pleasure of anyone else…

LUCIUS SENECA, *LETTERS FROM A STOIC*, "LIII. THE GREAT POWER AND VALUE OF PHILOSOPHY" (FROM C. 63-65 CE)

DETACHMENT

No one can have at all times what he pleases, but it is always in a man's power to have no mind to that which he knows he cannot have and cheerfully to make use of what he has.

LUCIUS SENECA, *LETTERS FROM A STOIC*, "CXXIII. ON LUXURY" (FROM C. 63-65 CE)

CHANGE

Death is such as generation is, a mystery of nature; a composition out of the same elements, and a decomposition into the same; and altogether not a thing of which any man should be ashamed, for it is not contrary to the nature of a reasonable animal, and not contrary to the reason of our constitution. It is natural that these things should be done by such persons, it is a matter of necessity; and if a man will not have it so, he will not allow the fig-tree to have juice. But by all means bear this in mind, that within a very short time both thou and he will be dead; and soon not even your names will be left behind.

MARCUS AURELIUS, *MEDITATIONS*, "BOOK IV" (FROM C. 180 CE)

VIRTUE

How hast thou behaved hitherto to the gods, thy parents, brethren, children, teachers, to those who looked after thy infancy, to thy friends, kinsfolk, to thy slaves? Consider if thou hast hitherto behaved to all in such a way that this may be said of thee: Never has wronged a man in deed or word.

MARCUS AURELIUS, *MEDITATIONS*, "BOOK V" (FROM C. 180 CE)

ACCEPTANCE

Whoever then clearly remembers this, that to man the measure of every act is the appearance (the opinion), whether the thing appears good or bad. If good, he is free from blame; if bad, himself suffers the penalty, for it is impossible that he who is deceived can be one person, and he who suffers another person – whoever remembers this will not be angry with any man, will not be vexed at any man, will not revile or blame any man, nor hate, nor quarrel with any man.

EPICTETUS, *THE TEACHINGS OF A STOIC: SELECTED DISCOURSES AND THE ENCHIRIDION*, "THAT WE OUGHT NOT TO BE ANGRY WITH MEN" (FROM C. EARLY 2ND CENTURY CE)

WISDOM

In short, if we observe, we shall find that the animal man is pained by nothing so much as by that which is irrational; and, on the contrary, attracted to nothing so much as to that which is rational.

EPICTETUS, *THE TEACHINGS OF A STOIC: SELECTED DISCOURSES AND THE ENCHIRIDION*, "HOW A MAN ON EVERY OCCASION CAN MAINTAIN HIS PROPER CHARACTER" (FROM C. EARLY 2ND CENTURY CE)

ACCEPTANCE

…there remains that which is peculiar to the good man, to be pleased and content with what happens, and with the thread which is spun for him; and not to defile the divinity which is planted in his breast, nor disturb it by a crowd of images, but to preserve it tranquil, following it obediently as a god, neither saying anything contrary to the truth, nor doing anything contrary to justice. And if all men refuse to believe that he lives a simple, modest, and contented life, he is neither angry with any of them, nor does he deviate from the way which leads to the end of life, to which a man ought to come pure, tranquil, ready to depart, and without any compulsion perfectly reconciled to his lot.

MARCUS AURELIUS, *MEDITATIONS*, "BOOK III" (FROM C. 180 CE)

TIME

Be not dissatisfied then that thou must live only so many years and not more; for as thou art satisfied with the amount of substance which has been assigned to thee, so be content with the time.

MARCUS AURELIUS, *MEDITATIONS*, "BOOK VI" (FROM C. 180 CE)

WISDOM

Would you know what true philosophy promiseth all mankind? I will tell you, good counsel. We see one man struggling in the jaws of death, another racked by poverty, another is tortured by riches – either his own or his neighbour's. One man dreads bad fortune, another is dissatisfied with good, one thinks himself hardly used by man, another by the gods. Seeing all this, why do you offer me such silly trifles as the abovementioned? Here is no room for jesting, you are called upon to succour the distressed, you are under an obligation to lend all possible assistance to the shipwrecked, to the prisoner, to the sick, to the poor and needy and to the unhappy under sentence of death.

LUCIUS SENECA, *LETTERS FROM A STOIC*, "XLVIII. ON SOCIAL VIRTUE AND THE TRIFLING OF SOPHISTRY" (FROM C. 63-65 CE)

VIRTUE

When thou hast been compelled by circumstances to be disturbed in a manner, quickly return to thyself and do not continue out of tune longer than the compulsion lasts; for thou wilt have more mastery over the harmony by continually recurring to it.

MARCUS AURELIUS, *MEDITATIONS*, "BOOK VI" (FROM C. 180 CE)

NOBILITY OF THOUGHT

Men seek retreats for themselves, houses in the country, seashores, and mountains; and thou too art wont to desire such things very much. But this is altogether a mark of the most common sort of men, for it is in thy power whenever thou shalt choose to retire into thyself. For nowhere either with more quiet or more freedom from trouble does a man retire than into his own soul, particularly when he has within him such thoughts that by looking into them he is immediately in perfect tranquility; and I affirm that tranquility is nothing else than the good ordering of the mind. Constantly then give to thyself this retreat, and renew thyself; and let thy principles be brief and fundamental, which, as soon as thou shalt recur to them, will be sufficient to cleanse the soul completely, and to send thee back free from all discontent with the things to which thou returnest.

MARCUS AURELIUS, *MEDITATIONS*, "BOOK IV" (FROM C. 180 CE)

GOODNESS

This man who has been mistaken and deceived about the most important things, and blinded, not in the faculty of vision which distinguishes white and black, but in the faculty which distinguishes good and bad, should we not destroy him? If you speak thus you will see how inhuman this is which you say, and that it is just as if you would say, Ought we not to destroy this blind and deaf man? But if the greatest harm is the privation of the greatest things, and the greatest thing in every man is the will or choice such as it ought to be, and a man is deprived of this will, why are you also angry with him? Man, you ought not to be affected contrary to nature by the bad things of another. Pity him rather; drop this readiness to be offended and to hate, and these words which the many utter: "These accursed and odious fellows." How have you been made so wise at once? Why then are we angry?

**EPICTETUS, *THE TEACHINGS OF A STOIC:
SELECTED DISCOURSES AND THE ENCHIRIDION*,
"THAT WE OUGHT NOT TO BE ANGRY WITH THE ERRORS
(FAULTS) OF OTHERS" (FROM C. EARLY 2ND CENTURY CE)**

CHANGE

Whatever this is that I am, it is a little flesh and breath, and the ruling part. Throw away thy books; no longer distract thyself: it is not allowed; but as if thou wast now dying, despise the flesh; it is blood and bones and a network, a contexture of nerves, veins, and arteries. See the breath also, what kind of a thing it is, air, and not always the same, but every moment sent out and again sucked in. The third then is the ruling part: consider thus: Thou art an old man; no longer let this be a slave, no longer be pulled by the strings like a puppet to unsocial movements, no longer either be dissatisfied with thy present lot, or shrink from the future.

MARCUS AURELIUS, *MEDITATIONS*, "BOOK II" (FROM C. 180 CE)

COOPERATION WITH NATURE

Does another do me wrong? Let him look to it. He has his own disposition, his own activity. I now have what the universal nature wills me to have; and I do what my nature now wills me to do.

MARCUS AURELIUS, *MEDITATIONS*, "BOOK V" (FROM C. 180 CE)

VIRTUE

...as an engraver when he has long been poring over his work and tired his eyes takes them off and gives them rest a while, in order to indulge and strengthen them, as they say, so we ought sometimes to unbend the mind and refresh it with certain amusements, not but that amusements may be work, and even from these due observation may pick out that may be turned to good account. This, my Lucilius, is what I practise myself; from whatever I read, however remote it may be, from philosophy I endeavour to extract something that may be useful.

LUCIUS SENECA, *LETTERS FROM A STOIC*, "LVIII. ON THE POVERTY OF THE LATIN TONGUE" (FROM C. 63-65 CE)

VIRTUE

Intercourse with the world is prejudicial; someone or other, either by example or discourse, will paint vice in such agreeable colours as to taint the mind insensibly, so that the more company we keep, the greater is our danger.

LUCIUS SENECA, *LETTERS FROM A STOIC*, "VII. ON PUBLIC SHOWS, PARTICULARLY THE GLADIATORS – AND CONVERSE WITH THE WORLD" (FROM C. 63-65 CE)

NOBILITY OF THOUGHT

God is reverenced and loved, love cannot accord with fear.

LUCIUS SENECA, *LETTERS FROM A STOIC*, "XLVII. ON TREATMENT OF SERVANTS" (FROM C. 63-65 CE)

VIRTUE

Will you not perceive either what you are, or what you were born for, or what this is for which you have received the faculty of sight? But you may say, There are some things disagreeable and troublesome in life… have you not received faculties by which you will be able to bear all that happens? Have you not received greatness of soul? Have you not received manliness? Have you not received endurance? And why do I trouble myself about anything that can happen if I possess greatness of soul? What shall distract my mind, or disturb me, or appear painful? Shall I not use the power for the purposes for which I received it, and shall I grieve and lament over what happens?

EPICTETUS, *THE TEACHINGS OF A STOIC: SELECTED DISCOURSES AND THE ENCHIRIDION*, "OF PROVIDENCE" (FROM C. EARLY 2ND CENTURY CE)

GOODNESS

You cannot imagine what new improvements I collect every day. Inform me, you say, of the means which you have experimentally found of so great efficacy. It is my desire so to do; I will transmit everything to you and am glad to learn in order to instruct. Nor indeed would anything give me pleasure, however excellent and salutary it might be, was I to keep the knowledge of it to myself. Was wisdom offered me under such restriction as to be obliged to conceal it, I would reject it. No enjoyment whatever can be agreeable without participation.

LUCIUS SENECA, *LETTERS FROM A STOIC*, "VI. ON FRIENDSHIP AND CONVERSATION" (FROM C. 63-65 CE)

VIRTUE

But he who values rational soul, a soul universal and fitted for political life, regards nothing else except this; and above all things he keeps his soul in a condition and in an activity conformable to reason and social life, and he cooperates to this end with those who are of the same kind as himself.

MARCUS AURELIUS, *MEDITATIONS*, "BOOK VI" (FROM C. 180 CE)

CHANGE

Remember to retire into this little territory of thy own, and above all do not distract or strain thyself, but be free, and look at things as a man, as a human being, as a citizen, as a mortal. But among the things readiest to thy hand to which thou shalt turn, let there be these, which are two. One is that things do not touch the soul, for they are external and remain immovable; but our perturbations come only from the opinion which is within. The other is that all these things, which thou seest, change immediately and will no longer be; and constantly bear in mind how many of these changes thou hast already witnessed. The universe is transformation: life is opinion.

MARCUS AURELIUS, *MEDITATIONS*, "BOOK IV" (FROM C. 180 CE)

TIME

What kind of people are those whom men wish to please, and for what objects, and by what kind of acts? How soon will time cover all things, and how many it has covered already.

MARCUS AURELIUS, *MEDITATIONS*, "BOOK VI" (FROM C. 180 CE)

GOODNESS

…remember that you are a son. What does this character promise? To consider that everything which is the son's belongs to the father, to obey him in all things, never to blame him to another, nor to say or do anything which does him injury, to yield to him in all things and give way, co-operating with him as far as you can. After this know that you are a brother also, and that to this character it is due to make concessions; to be easily persuaded, to speak good of your brother, never to claim in opposition to him any of the things which are independent of the will, but readily to give them up, that you may have the larger share in what is dependent on the will. For see what a thing it is, in place of a lettuce, if it should so happen, or a seat, to gain for yourself goodness of disposition. How great is the advantage.

EPICTETUS, *THE TEACHINGS OF A STOIC: SELECTED DISCOURSES AND THE ENCHIRIDION*, "HOW WE MAY DISCOVER THE DUTIES OF LIFE FROM NAMES" (FROM C. EARLY 2ND CENTURY CE)

NOBILITY OF THOUGHT

We ought then to check in the series of our thoughts everything that is without a purpose and useless, but most of all the overcurious feeling and the malignant…

MARCUS AURELIUS, *MEDITATIONS*, "BOOK III" (FROM C. 180 CE)

WISDOM

…when full of wine he yet thirsted for blood. It would have been intolerable in him to have done what he did had he been sober, but how much more intolerable was it for him to do these horrid things in a drunken riot? Cruelty commonly attends upon drunkenness, for the sanity of the mind is hereby disturbed and exasperated. As long diseases make the eyes so weak as not to endure the least glimpse of the fun, so a habit of drunkenness weakens the mind, for as men are often not masters of themselves, being inured to such vices as are conceived by lavish drinking they are apt to perpetrate the fame without the instigation of wine.

LUCIUS SENECA, *LETTERS FROM A STOIC*, "LXXIX. ON DRUNKENNESS" (FROM C. 63-65 CE)

TIME

86

For with what art thou discontented? With the badness of men? Recall to thy mind this conclusion, that rational animals exist for one another, and that to endure is a part of justice, and that men do wrong involuntarily; and consider how many already, after mutual enmity, suspicion, hatred, and fighting, have been stretched dead, reduced to ashes; and be quiet at last...

MARCUS AURELIUS, *MEDITATIONS*, "BOOK IV" (FROM C. 180 CE)

ACCEPTANCE

87

Tell me where I can escape death; discover for me the country, show me the men to whom I must go, whom death does not visit. Discover to me a charm against death. If I have not one, what do you wish me to do? I cannot escape from death. Shall I not escape from the fear of death, but shall I die lamenting and trembling? For the origin of perturbation is this, to wish for something, and that this should not happen.

EPICTETUS, *THE TEACHINGS OF A STOIC:
SELECTED DISCOURSES AND THE ENCHIRIDION*,
"HOW WE SHOULD STRUGGLE WITH CIRCUMSTANCES"
(FROM C. EARLY 2ND CENTURY CE)

ACCEPTANCE

But now because we do not know the future, it is our duty to stick to the things which are in their nature more suitable for our choice, for we were made, among other things, for this.

EPICTETUS, *THE TEACHINGS OF A STOIC: SELECTED DISCOURSES AND THE ENCHIRIDION*, "HOW WE MAY DISCOVER THE DUTIES OF LIFE FROM NAMES" (FROM C. EARLY 2ND CENTURY CE)

DETACHMENT

Go and salute a certain person. How? Not meanly. But I have been shut out, for I have not learned to make my way through the window; and when I have found the door shut, I must either come back or enter through the window. But still speak to him. In what way? Not meanly. But suppose that you have not got what you wanted. Was this your business, and not his? Why then do you claim that which belongs to another? Always remember what is your own, and what belongs to another; and you will not be disturbed.

EPICTETUS, *THE TEACHINGS OF A STOIC: SELECTED DISCOURSES AND THE ENCHIRIDION*, "OF INDIFFERENCE" (FROM C. EARLY 2ND CENTURY CE)

ACCEPTANCE

…to be instructed is this, to learn to wish that everything may happen as it does. And how do things happen? As the disposer has disposed them? And he has appointed summer and winter, and abundance and scarcity, and virtue and vice, and all such opposites for the harmony of the whole; and to each of us he has given a body, and parts of the body, and possessions, and companions… But you are unwilling to endure, and are discontented; and if you are alone, you call it solitude; and if you are with men, you call them knaves and robbers; and you find fault with your own parents and children, and brothers and neighbours. But you ought when you are alone to call this condition by the name of tranquillity and freedom, and to think yourself like to the gods; and when you are with many, you ought not to call it crowd, nor trouble, nor uneasiness, but festival and assembly, and so accept all contentedly.

EPICTETUS, *THE TEACHINGS OF A STOIC: SELECTED DISCOURSES AND THE ENCHIRIDION*, "OF CONTENTMENT" (FROM C. EARLY 2ND CENTURY CE)

WISDOM

The wise man dreads no accident, he is satisfied in himself. But this quality, my Lucilius, is generally misinterpreted, men are apt to exclude the wise man from all community with the world, contracting him, as it were, within his own skin. It will be proper therefore to distinguish and explain what we mean by self-complacency. Now, a wise man is satisfied in himself not merely with regard to life, but to his living happily, the former indeed wants many things, but the latter nothing more than a sound, elevated mind, contemptuous of the power of fortune.

LUCIUS SENECA, *LETTERS FROM A STOIC*, "IX. ON FRIENDSHIP, SELF-COMPLACENCY AND CONTENTMENT" (FROM C. 63-65 CE)

VIRTUE

Or if one or two of better parts than ordinary should by chance fall in your way, it will demand some pains to instruct them and bring them to your taste. "For whom, then," you will say, "have you taken so much pains to learn?" Fear not, your time was not thrown away if it was for yourself only.

LUCIUS SENECA, *LETTERS FROM A STOIC*, "VII. ON PUBLIC SHOWS, PARTICULARLY THE GLADIATORS - AND CONVERSE WITH THE WORLD" (FROM C. 63-65 CE)

WISDOM

What is true, Lucilius, is my own. And I shall go on in quoting Epicurus and others, that they who enlist themselves in any sect and regard not *what* is said but by *whom* it is said may know that, when anything is said perfectly good, all the world have a right to it.

LUCIUS SENECA, *LETTERS FROM A STOIC*, "XII. ON LIFE AND OLD AGE" (FROM C. 63-65 CE)

GOODNESS

Plato and Aristotle, and the whole tribe of philosophers of various sects, learned more from the morals of Socrates than from his preachments. It was not the school of Epicurus but familiarity that made Metrodorus, Hermachus and Polyaenus so eminent in the world. Nor do I invite you hither merely for your good but my own, as in conference each may assist the other in many points.

LUCIUS SENECA, *LETTERS FROM A STOIC*, "VI. ON FRIENDSHIP AND CONVERSATION" (FROM C. 63-65 CE)

COOPERATION WITH NATURE

…everything which belongs to the body is a stream, and what belongs to the soul is a dream and vapour, and life is a warfare and a stranger's sojourn, and after-fame is oblivion. What then is that which is able to conduct a man? One thing and only one, philosophy. But this consists in keeping the daemon within a man free from violence and unharmed, superior to pains and pleasures, doing nothing without purpose, nor yet falsely and with hypocrisy, not feeling the need of another man's doing or not doing anything; and besides, accepting all that happens, and all that is allotted, as coming from thence, wherever it is, from whence he himself came; and, finally, waiting for death with a cheerful mind, as being nothing else than a dissolution of the elements of which every living being is compounded. But if there is no harm to the elements themselves in each continually changing into another, why should a man have any apprehension about the change and dissolution of all the elements? For it is according to nature, and nothing is evil which is according to nature.

MARCUS AURELIUS, *MEDITATIONS*, "BOOK II" (FROM C. 180 CE)

ACCEPTANCE

And here we conceive the work of a philosopher to be something of this kind: he must adapt his wish to what is going on, so that neither any of the things which are taking place shall take place contrary to our wish, nor any of the things which do not take place shall not take place when we wish that they should. From this the result is to those who have so arranged the work of philosophy, not to fail in the desire, nor to fall in with that which they would avoid; without uneasiness, without fear, without perturbation to pass through life themselves, together with their associates maintaining the relations both natural and acquired, as the relation of son, of father, of brother, of citizen, of man, of wife, of neighbour, of fellow-traveller, of ruler, of ruled. The work of a philosopher we conceive to be something like this.

EPICTETUS, *THE TEACHINGS OF A STOIC: SELECTED DISCOURSES AND THE ENCHIRIDION*, "TO NASO" (FROM C. EARLY 2ND CENTURY CE)

DETACHMENT

Never value anything as profitable to thyself which shall compel thee to break thy promise, to lose thy self respect, to hate any man, to suspect, to curse, to act the hypocrite, to desire anything which needs walls and curtains: for he who has preferred to everything intelligence and daemon and the worship of its excellence, acts no tragic part, does not groan, will not need either solitude or much company; and, what is chief of all, he will live without either pursuing or flying from death; but whether for a longer or a shorter time he shall have the soul enclosed in the body, he cares not at all: for even if he must depart immediately, he will go as readily as if he were going to do anything else which can be done with decency and order; taking care of this only all through life, that his thoughts turn not away from anything which belongs to an intelligent animal and a member of a civil community.

MARCUS AURELIUS, *MEDITATIONS*, "BOOK III"
(FROM C. 180 CE)

NOBILITY OF THOUGHT

98

…know that if you think anyone your friend whom you dare not trust as far as you would your own self, you are greatly mistaken and know not the importance of true friendship. It may be necessary to consult and advise with a friend in everything, but it is proper first to know him. After friendship is contracted all trust is due, but a judicious choice must precede it.

LUCIUS SENECA, *LETTERS FROM A STOIC*, "III. ON FRIENDSHIP" (FROM C. 63-65 CE)

CHANGE

99

…live so with an inferior as you would have a superior live with you. As often as you think on the power you have over a servant, reflect on the power your master has over you. But you say you have no master?

Be it so, the world goes well at present, it may not do so always. You may one day be a servant yourself.

LUCIUS SENECA, *LETTERS FROM A STOIC*, "XLVII. ON TREATMENT OF SERVANTS" (FROM C. 63-65 CE)

DETACHMENT

100

Is any man then afraid about things which are not evils? No. Is he afraid about things which are evils, but still so far within his power that they may not happen? Certainly he is not. If then the things which are independent of the will are neither good nor bad, and all things which do depend on the will are within our power, and no man can either take them from us or give them to us, if we do not choose, where is room left for anxiety? But we are anxious about our poor body, our little property, about the will of Cæsar; but not anxious about things internal. Are we anxious about not forming a false opinion? No, for this is in my power. About not exerting our movements contrary to nature? No, not even about this.

EPICTETUS, *THE TEACHINGS OF A STOIC: SELECTED DISCOURSES AND THE ENCHIRIDION*, "ON ANXIETY (SOLICITUDE)" (FROM C. EARLY 2ND CENTURY CE)

VIRTUE

101

Since it is possible that thou mayest depart from life this very moment, regulate every act and thought accordingly.

MARCUS AURELIUS, *MEDITATIONS*, "BOOK II" (FROM C. 180 CE)

TIME

Our whole time consists of parts and circles circumscribed within circles of different dimensions, someone of which takes in and compareth the rest. And this is what includes the life of man. Another compareth the years of youth and another those of childhood. There is also a complete year, which contains in itself all those times that by multiplication form the course of life. A month is confined in still-narrower bounds, and a day consists of yet a smaller compass. And this hath also a beginning and ending, a circuit from east to west.

LUCIUS SENECA, *LETTERS FROM A STOIC*, "XII. ON LIFE AND OLD AGE" (FROM C. 63-65 CE)

ACCEPTANCE

Adapt thyself to the things with which thy lot has been cast: and the men among whom thou hast received thy portion, love them, but do it truly, sincerely.

MARCUS AURELIUS, *MEDITATIONS*, "BOOK VI" (FROM C. 180 CE)

VIRTUE

If thou workest at that which is before thee, following right reason seriously, vigorously, calmly, without allowing anything else to distract thee, but keeping thy divine part pure, as if thou shouldst be bound to give it back immediately; if thou holdest to this, expecting nothing, fearing nothing, but satisfied with thy present activity according to nature, and with heroic truth in every word and sound which thou utterest, thou wilt live happy. And there is no man who is able to prevent this.

MARCUS AURELIUS, *MEDITATIONS*, "BOOK III"
(FROM C. 180 CE)

GOODNESS

Hecaton today gave me great pleasure: "Do you ask," says he, "what improvement I have made of late? I have learned to be a friend to myself." Great improvement this indeed! Such a one can never be said to be alone, for know that he who is a friend to himself is a friend to all mankind.

LUCIUS SENECA, *LETTERS FROM A STOIC*, "VI. ON
FRIENDSHIP AND CONVERSATION" (FROM C. 63-65 CE)

DETACHMENT

And what is the divine law? To keep a man's own, not to claim that which belongs to others, but to use what is given, and when it is not given, not to desire it; and when a thing is taken away, to give it up readily and immediately, and to be thankful for the time that a man has had the use of it…

EPICTETUS, *THE TEACHINGS OF A STOIC: SELECTED DISCOURSES AND THE ENCHIRIDION*, "THAT WE DO NOT STRIVE TO USE OUR OPINIONS ABOUT GOOD AND EVIL" (FROM C. EARLY 2ND CENTURY CE)

TIME

…bear in mind that every man lives only this present time, which is an indivisible point, and that all the rest of his life is either past or it is uncertain. Short then is the time which every man lives, and small the nook of the earth where he lives; and short too the longest posthumous fame, and even this only continued by a succession of poor human beings, who will very soon die, and who know not even themselves, much less him who died long ago.

MARCUS AURELIUS, *MEDITATIONS*, "BOOK III" (FROM C. 180 CE)

TIME

Heraclitus [remarked], "one day is par to another." This some interpret as if he had said, "They are equal with regard to hours," which is certainly true, for if a day consists of twenty-four hours, every day is equal, for what is lost in the day is made up in the night. Others interpret it that one day is equal to any other by way of resemblance, as the longest space of time exhibits no more than what you have seen in one day, viz. light and darkness, frequently repeated in the alternate changes of the heavens, and is not otherwise different than in not being always of an equal length. Every day, therefore, is to be so ordered and regulated, as if it closed the rear, set bounds to and completed life.

LUCIUS SENECA, *LETTERS FROM A STOIC*, "XII. ON LIFE AND OLD AGE" (FROM C. 63-65 CE)

VIRTUE

For universally, be not deceived, every animal is attached to nothing so much as to its own interests. Whatever then appears to it an impediment to this interest, whether this be a brother, or a father, or a child, or beloved, or lover, it hates, spurns, curses; for its nature is to love nothing so much as its own interests: this is father, and brother, and kinsman, and country, and God. When then the gods appear to us to be an impediment to this, we abuse them and throw down their statues and burn their temples, as Alexander ordered the temples of Aesculapius to be burned when his dear friend died. For this reason, if a man put in the same place his interest, sanctity, goodness, and country, and parents, and friends, all these are secured: but if he puts in one place his interest, in another his friends, and his country and his kinsmen and justice itself, all these give way, being borne down by the weight of interest.

EPICTETUS, *THE TEACHINGS OF A STOIC:*
SELECTED DISCOURSES AND THE ENCHIRIDION,
"ON FRIENDSHIP" (FROM C. EARLY 2ND CENTURY CE)

CHANGE

...I am put in mind of my old age. Be it so, let me enjoy it, let me love it. It is replete with pleasure when we know how to use it. Fruit is then more grateful when at the end of the season. The bloom of youth is then most comely when passing into manhood. Your wine-bibbers relish best the last bottle, even that which oversets them and gives the finishing stroke to the debauch. Whatever is exquisite in pleasure is reserved to the last. Even age is most pleasant when the decay is not too rapid but comes gently on, nor can I think it destitute of pleasure even on the verge of life. Or this may be reckoned instead of pleasure that it wants none. How sweet is life when all anxious desires have taken their leave of us!

LUCIUS SENECA, *LETTERS FROM A STOIC*, "XII. ON LIFE AND OLD AGE" (FROM C. 63-65 CE)

TIME

Everything is only for a day, both that which remembers and that which is remembered.

MARCUS AURELIUS, *MEDITATIONS*, "BOOK IV" (FROM C. 180 CE)

NOBILITY OF THOUGHT

A friend is to be enjoyed by the mind, this is never absent, it daily sees whom it pleases. Therefore, still study with me, sup with me, walk with me; we should live in very narrow bounds could anything be excluded our thoughts. I see you still, my Lucilius, I ever hear thee. In short, I am so much with you that I am in doubt whether I shall send you any more epistles or only a complemental billet.

LUCIUS SENECA, *LETTERS FROM A STOIC*, "LV. A TRUE FRIEND IS NEVER ABSENT" (FROM C. 63-65 CE)

VIRTUE

…divine providence is pleased to deliver the world (not less mortal than ourselves) from danger and destruction, our own care and forecast may in some measure contribute to prolong our days and keep up this little tenement, provided we can govern and restrain the fond passions that bring untimely ruin on the greater part of mankind.

LUCIUS SENECA, *LETTERS FROM A STOIC*, "LVIII. ON THE POVERTY OF THE LATIN TONGUE" (FROM C. 63-65 CE)

ACCEPTANCE

This is why the ancients taught the maxim, Know thyself. Therefore we ought to exercise ourselves in small things, and beginning with them to proceed to the greater. I have pain in the head. Do not say, Alas! I have pain in the ear. Do not say alas! And I do not say that you are not allowed to groan, but do not groan inwardly; and if your slave is slow in bringing a bandage, do not cry out and torment yourself, and say, Everybody hates me; for who would not hate such a man? For the future, relying on these opinions, walk about upright, free; not trusting to the size of your body, as an athlete, for a man ought not to be invincible in the way that an ass is.

EPICTETUS, *THE TEACHINGS OF A STOIC: SELECTED DISCOURSES AND THE ENCHIRIDION*, "THAT WE OUGHT NOT TO BE ANGRY WITH THE ERRORS (FAULTS) OF OTHERS" (FROM C. EARLY 2ND CENTURY CE)

COOPERATION WITH NATURE

In conformity to the nature of the universe every single thing is accomplished…

MARCUS AURELIUS, *MEDITATIONS*, "BOOK VI" (FROM C. 180 CE)

WISDOM

But philosophy, my Lucilius, is so sacred and venerable a thing that whatever pretends to be like it must rest upon a falsity. For the vulgar think a man who has retired from business must necessarily be free from all care and trouble, well satisfied in and living altogether for himself. Whereas nothing like this can be applied to anyone but to the wise man, he indeed is a stranger to anxiety and knows how to live for himself. Such a one, I say (which is the principal good) knows how to live, whereas the man who flies from men and business, whom the ill success of his ambition hath banished from conversation, who cannot bear to see another happier than himself, who like a timorous and silly animal hides himself for fear, such a one lives not to himself but to luxury, to deep, to lust. He lives not always to himself who lives to no one else. Yet there is something so valuable in constancy and perseverance that even the most stubborn indolence gains some credit.

LUCIUS SENECA, *LETTERS FROM A STOIC*, "LV. A TRUE FRIEND IS NEVER ABSENT" (FROM C. 63-65 CE)

GOODNESS

Observe then as thou hast begun; and whatever thou doest, do it in conjunction with this, the being good, and in the sense in which a man is properly understood to be good. Keep to this in every action. Do not have such an opinion of things as he has who does thee wrong, or such as he wishes thee to have, but look at them as they are in truth.

MARCUS AURELIUS, *MEDITATIONS*, "BOOK IV"
(FROM C. 180 CE)

WILL

Even rest itself is sometimes restless, and therefore it is proper we should be roused to action and employed in some of the liberal sciences as often as listlessness seizes us impatient of its own weight. Great generals when they see a soldier disobedient to orders condemn him to some hard labour… They have no time to play. And wanton who are tied down to business, and nothing is more certain than that the vices of idleness are thrown off by proper employ.

LUCIUS SENECA, *LETTERS FROM A STOIC*, "LVI.
ON TRANQUILLITY" (FROM C. 63-65 CE)

WISDOM

A man should always have these two rules in readiness; the one, to do only whatever the reason of the ruling and legislating faculty may suggest for the use of men; the other, to change thy opinion, if there is anyone at hand who sets thee right and moves thee from any opinion. But this change of opinion must proceed only from a certain persuasion, as of what is just or of common advantage, and the like, not because it appears pleasant or brings reputation. Hast thou reason? I have – why then dost not thou use it? For if this does its own work, what else dost thou wish? Thou hast existed as a part.

MARCUS AURELIUS, *MEDITATIONS*, "BOOK IV" (FROM C. 180 CE)

TIME

For what is a master? Man is not the master of man; but death is, and life and pleasure and pain; for if he comes without these things, bring Cæsar to me and you will see how firm I am.

EPICTETUS, *THE TEACHINGS OF A STOIC: SELECTED DISCOURSES AND THE ENCHIRIDION*, "ON CONSTANCY (OR FIRMNESS)" (FROM C. EARLY 2ND CENTURY CE)

DETACHMENT

Accept also of a nice distinction made by Chrysippus, he affirms that "a wise man can want nothing, yet many things are necessary for him." On the contrary, "a fool stands not in need of anything, for there is nothing he knows how to use, but he wants everything." The wise man stands in need of eyes and hands and other requisites for daily use, but he wants nothing, for to want is to be necessitous but a wise man is a stranger to necessity. However satisfied, therefore, he may be in himself, he may still make use of a friend, nor does he act against principle if he desires more than one, not that he thereby may live happily for he can be happy without a friend. The *summum bonum* seeks not any external provision, it is maintained within and is entire in itself. If it looks out for any foreign accession it becomes subject to the caprice of fortune.

LUCIUS SENECA, *LETTERS FROM A STOIC*, "IX. ON FRIENDSHIP, SELF-COMPLACENCY AND CONTENTMENT" (FROM C. 63-65 CE)

WILL

The being (nature) of the good is a certain will; the being of the bad is a certain kind of will. What, then, are externals? Materials for the will, about which the will being conversant shall obtain its own good or evil. How shall it obtain the good? If it does not admire (over-value) the materials; for the opinions about the materials, if the opinions are right, make the will good: but perverse and distorted opinions make the will bad. God has fixed this law, and says, "If you would have anything good, receive it from yourself." You say, No, but I will have it from another. Do not so: but receive it from yourself.

EPICTETUS, *THE TEACHINGS OF A STOIC: SELECTED DISCOURSES AND THE ENCHIRIDION*, "ON CONSTANCY (OR FIRMNESS)" (FROM C. EARLY 2ND CENTURY CE)

DETACHMENT

I do my duty: other things trouble me not; for they are either things without life, or things without reason, or things that have rambled and know not the way.

MARCUS AURELIUS, *MEDITATIONS*, "BOOK VI" (FROM C. 180 CE)

DETACHMENT

He is collected within himself, there he dwells and, notwithstanding, so long as it is in his power, he orders and busies himself with worldly affairs, he is contented in himself, he marries a wife, still contented, he brings up his children, still contented, and perhaps had rather not live at all than live without a companion. It is not, however, with a view to advantage that invites him to cultivate friendship, but a sort of instinct or natural inclination.

LUCIUS SENECA, *LETTERS FROM A STOIC*, "IX. ON FRIENDSHIP, SELF-COMPLACENCY AND CONTENTMENT" (FROM C. 63-65 CE)

GOODNESS

God is near thee, he is with thee. Yes, Lucilius, I say, a holy spirit resides within us, the observer of good and evil and our constant guardian. And as we treat him, he treats us. At least no good man is without a God. Could anyone ever rise above the power of fortune without his assistance? It is he that inspires us with thoughts, upright, just and pure.

LUCIUS SENECA, *LETTERS FROM A STOIC*, "XLI. THERE IS A CERTAIN DIVINITY IN GOOD MEN" (FROM C. 63-65 CE)

DETACHMENT

How quickly all things disappear, in the universe the bodies themselves, but in time the remembrance of them; what is the nature of all sensible things, and particularly those which attract with the bait of pleasure or terrify by pain, or are noised abroad by vapoury fame; how worthless, and contemptible, and sordid, and perishable, and dead they are – all this it is the part of the intellectual faculty to observe. To observe too who these are whose opinions and voices give reputation; what death is, and the fact that, if a man looks at it in itself, and by the abstractive power of reflection resolves into their parts all the things which present themselves to the imagination in it, he will then consider it to be nothing else than an operation of nature; and if anyone is afraid of an operation of nature, he is a child. This, however, is not only an operation of nature, but it is also a thing which conduces to the purposes of nature.

MARCUS AURELIUS, *MEDITATIONS*, "BOOK II" (FROM C. 180 CE)

CHANGE

...rejoice in that which is present and be content with the things which come in season. If you see anything which you have learned and inquired about occurring to you in your course of life (or opportunely applied by you to the acts of life), be delighted at it... if you are not moved by what you formerly were, and not in the same way as you once were, you can celebrate a festival daily – today because you have behaved well in one act, and tomorrow because you have behaved well in another.

EPICTETUS, *THE TEACHINGS OF A STOIC: SELECTED DISCOURSES AND THE ENCHIRIDION*, "TO THOSE WHO ARE DESIROUS OF PASSING LIFE IN TRANQUILITY" (FROM C. EARLY 2ND CENTURY CE)

GOODNESS

Look within. Within is the fountain of good, and it will ever bubble up, if thou wilt ever dig.

MARCUS AURELIUS, *MEDITATIONS*, "BOOK VII" (FROM C. 180 CE)

NOBILITY OF THOUGHT

"He who does not think himself happy is miserable, though he command the world." And that you may know this to be the common voice of nature, you will find is the comic poet; "he is not blessed who thinks himself not blessed." It matters not what condition you are in, if you think it a bad one. What if that villainously rich man or that lord of many, but slave to more, call themselves happy, will this their declaration make them so? No. It avails not what a man says of himself but what he thinks, nor what he thinks today but continually. Nor need you be concerned that anyone hath amassed great wealth which he is unworthy of, for no one but the wise man is capable of self-complacency, and a fool will be disgusted at his own condition, be it what it will.

LUCIUS SENECA, *LETTERS FROM A STOIC*, "IX. ON FRIENDSHIP, SELF-COMPLACENCY AND CONTENTMENT" (FROM C. 63-65 CE)

WILL

But if you ask me what then is the most excellent of all things, what must I say? I cannot say the power of speaking, but the power of the will, when it is right. For it is this which uses the other (the power of speaking), and all the other faculties both small and great. For when this faculty of the will is set right, a man who is not good becomes good: but when it fails, a man becomes bad. It is through this that we are unfortunate, that we are fortunate, that we blame one another, are pleased with one another. In a word, it is this which if we neglect it makes unhappiness, and if we carefully look after it, makes happiness.

EPICTETUS, *THE TEACHINGS OF A STOIC: SELECTED DISCOURSES AND THE ENCHIRIDION*, "ON THE POWER OF SPEAKING" (FROM C. EARLY 2ND CENTURY CE)

TIME

These two things then thou must bear in mind; the one, that all things from eternity are of like forms and come round in a circle, and that it makes no difference whether a man shall see the same things during a hundred years or two hundred, or an infinite time; and the second, that the longest liver and he who will die soonest lose just the same. For the present is the only thing of which a man can be deprived, if it is true that this is the only thing which he has, and that a man cannot lose a thing if he has it not.

MARCUS AURELIUS, *MEDITATIONS*, "BOOK II" (FROM C. 180 CE)

NOBILITY OF THOUGHT

Learn my opinions: show me yours; and then say that you have visited me. Let us examine one another: if I have any bad opinion, take it away; if you have any, show it. This is the meaning of meeting with a philosopher.

EPICTETUS, *THE TEACHINGS OF A STOIC: SELECTED DISCOURSES AND THE ENCHIRIDION*, "TO A CERTAIN RHETORICIAN WHO WAS GOING UP TO ROME ON A SUIT" (FROM C. EARLY 2ND CENTURY CE)

CHANGE

…frugality and temperance are, no doubt, the great preservatives of old age, which, as I think it is not greatly to be coveted, is not to be refused. It is pleasant to dwell as long as possible with one's self, especially when a man has rendered himself worthy of self-enjoyment. Therefore, let us examine this point, whether it be right to disdain the extremities of old age and not wait the issue but forcibly close the scene. He is not far from a coward who chooses to linger out his fate, as a man must be a sot who drains the pitcher and drinks up the very dregs, yet this must likewise be enquired into, whether the last stage of life can properly be called the dregs and whether it may not be the most pure and clearest part of it, at least if the intellect hath received no injury, and the senses, still perfect, entertain the mind or the body hath no paralytic disorder or other extraordinary defect.

LUCIUS SENECA, *LETTERS FROM A STOIC*, "LVIII. ON THE POVERTY OF THE LATIN TONGUE" (FROM C. 63-65 CE)

COOPERATION WITH NATURE

134

The soul of man does violence to itself, first of all, when it becomes an abscess and, as it were, a tumour on the universe, so far as it can. For to be vexed at anything which happens is a separation of ourselves from nature, in some part of which the natures of all other things are contained. In the next place, the soul does violence to itself when it turns away from any man, or even moves towards him with the intention of injuring, such as are the souls of those who are angry. In the third place, the soul does violence to itself when it is overpowered by pleasure or by pain. Fourthly, when it plays a part, and does or says anything insincerely and untruly. Fifthly, when it allows any act of its own and any movement to be without an aim, and does anything thoughtlessly and without considering what it is, it being right that even the smallest things be done with reference to an end; and the end of rational animals is to follow the reason…

MARCUS AURELIUS, *MEDITATIONS*, "BOOK II"
(FROM C. 180 CE)

WILL

For if you wish to maintain a will conformable to nature, you have every security, every facility, you have no troubles. For if you wish to maintain what is in your own power and is naturally free, and if you are content with these, what else do you care for? For who is the master of such things? Who can take them away? If you choose to be modest and faithful, who shall not allow you to be so? If you choose not to be restrained or compelled, who shall compel you to desire what you think that you ought not to desire? Who shall compel you to avoid what you do not think fit to avoid?

EPICTETUS, *THE TEACHINGS OF A STOIC: SELECTED DISCOURSES AND THE ENCHIRIDION*, "OF TRANQUILITY (FREEDOM FROM PERTURBATION)" (FROM C. EARLY 2ND CENTURY CE)

VIRTUE

Above, below, all around are the movements of the elements. But the motion of virtue is in none of these: it is something more divine, and advancing by a way hardly observed it goes happily on its road.

MARCUS AURELIUS, *MEDITATIONS*, "BOOK VI" (FROM C. 180 CE)

COOPERATION WITH NATURE

It is no common (easy) thing to do this only, to fulfil the promise of a man's nature. For what is a man? The answer is, A rational and mortal being. Then by the rational faculty from whom are we separated? From wild beasts. And from what others? From sheep and like animals. Take care then to do nothing like a wild beast; but if you do, you have lost the character of a man; you have not fulfilled your promise. See that you do nothing like a sheep; but if you do, in this case also the man is lost. What then do we do as sheep? When we act gluttonously, when we act lewdly, when we act rashly, filthily, inconsiderately, to what have we declined? To sheep. What have we lost? The rational faculty. When we act contentiously and harmfully and passionately and violently, to what have we declined? To wild beasts.

EPICTETUS, *THE TEACHINGS OF A STOIC: SELECTED DISCOURSES AND THE ENCHIRIDION*, "THAT WHEN WE CANNOT FULFIL THAT WHICH THE CHARACTER OF A MAN PROMISES, WE ASSUME THE CHARACTER OF A PHILOSOPHER" (FROM C. EARLY 2ND CENTURY CE)

COOPERATION WITH NATURE

How, even if my brother is not reconciled to me, shall I maintain myself in a state conformable to nature? Nothing great, said Epictetus, is produced suddenly, since not even the grape or the fig is. If you say to me now that you want a fig, I will answer to you that it requires time: let it flower first, then put forth fruit, and then ripen. Is then the fruit of a fig-tree not perfected suddenly and in one hour, and would you possess the fruit of a man's mind in so short a time and so easily? Do not expect it, even if I tell you.

EPICTETUS, *THE TEACHINGS OF A STOIC: SELECTED DISCOURSES AND THE ENCHIRIDION*, "WHAT PHILOSOPHY PROMISES" (FROM C. EARLY 2ND CENTURY CE)

WILL

Things themselves touch not the soul, not in the least degree; nor have they admission to the soul, nor can they turn or move the soul: but the soul turns and moves itself alone, and whatever judgements it may think proper to make, such it makes for itself the things which present themselves to it.

MARCUS AURELIUS, *MEDITATIONS*, "BOOK V" (FROM C. 180 CE)

WILL

Show those qualities then which are altogether in thy power, sincerity, gravity, endurance of labour, aversion to pleasure, contentment with thy portion and with few things, benevolence, frankness, no love of superfluity, freedom from trifling magnanimity. Dost thou not see how many qualities thou art immediately able to exhibit, in which there is no excuse of natural incapacity and unfitness, and yet thou still remainest voluntarily below the mark? Or art thou compelled through being defectively furnished by nature to murmur, and to be stingy, and to flatter, and to find fault with thy poor body, and to try to please men, and to make great display, and to be so restless in thy mind? No, by the gods: but thou mightest have been delivered from these things long ago. Only if in truth thou canst be charged with being rather slow and dull of comprehension, thou must exert thyself about this also, not neglecting it nor yet taking pleasure in thy dullness.

MARCUS AURELIUS, *MEDITATIONS*, "BOOK V" (FROM C. 180 CE)

WISDOM

I can only say this to you, that he who knows not who he is, and for what purpose he exists, and what is this world, and with whom he is associated, and what things are the good and the bad, and the beautiful and the ugly, and who neither understands discourse nor demonstration, nor what is true nor what is false, and who is not able to distinguish them, will neither desire according to nature nor turn away nor move towards, nor intend (to act), nor assent, nor dissent, nor suspend his judgment: to say all in a few words, he will go about dumb and blind, thinking that he is somebody, but being nobody. Is this so now for the first time? Is it not the fact that ever since the human race existed, all errors and misfortunes have arisen through this ignorance?

EPICTETUS, *THE TEACHINGS OF A STOIC: SELECTED DISCOURSES AND THE ENCHIRIDION*, "TO (OR AGAINST) A PERSON WHO WAS ONE OF THOSE WHO WERE NOT VALUED (ESTEEMED) BY HIM" (FROM C. EARLY 2ND CENTURY CE)

CHANGE

Socrates, to one complaining after the fame manner, says, "why do you wonder that travelling does you no good when, go where you will, you carry yourself along with you?" The same cause that sent you out still at heart. What can the novelty of foreign lands avail? What the knowledge of diverse cities and countries? It is all a fruitless labour. And do you ask why this your flight is to so little purpose? It is because, as Socrates said, "you cannot fly from yourself." The mind's burden must be left behind or you will nowhere find complacency and delight.

LUCIUS SENECA, *LETTERS FROM A STOIC*, "XXVIII. CHANGE OF PLACE MAKES NO ALTERATION IN THE MIND" (FROM C. 63-65 CE)

NOBILITY OF THOUGHT

Such as are thy habitual thoughts, such also will be the character of thy mind; for the soul is dyed by the thoughts. Dye it then with a continuous series of such thoughts as these: for instance, that where a man can live, there he can also live well.

MARCUS AURELIUS, *MEDITATIONS*, "BOOK V" (FROM C. 180 CE)

ACCEPTANCE

For two reasons then it is right to be content with that which happens to thee; the one, because it was done for thee and prescribed for thee, and in a manner had reference to thee, originally from the most ancient causes spun with thy destiny; and the other, because even that which comes severally to every man is to the power which administers the universe a cause of felicity and perfection, nay even of its very continuance. For the integrity of the whole is mutilated, if thou cuttest off anything whatever from the conjunction and the continuity either of the parts or of the causes. And thou dost cut off, as far as it is in thy power, when thou art dissatisfied, and in a manner triest to put anything out of the way.

MARCUS AURELIUS, *MEDITATIONS*, "BOOK V" (FROM C. 180 CE)

WISDOM

…if any man is able to convince me and show me that I do not think or act right, I will gladly change; for I seek the truth by which no man was ever injured. But he is injured who abides in his error and ignorance.

MARCUS AURELIUS, *MEDITATIONS*, "BOOK VI" (FROM C. 180 CE)

WISDOM

146

Observe whom you yourself praise, when you praise many persons without partiality: do you praise the just or the unjust? The just. Whether do you praise the moderate or the immoderate? The moderate. And the temperate or the intemperate? The temperate. If then you make yourself such a person, you will know that you will make yourself beautiful; but so long as you neglect these things, you must be ugly, even though you contrive all you can to appear beautiful.

EPICTETUS, *THE TEACHINGS OF A STOIC: SELECTED DISCOURSES AND THE ENCHIRIDION*, "OF FINERY IN DRESS" (FROM C. EARLY 2ND CENTURY CE)

CHANGE

147

"…not to yield to affliction nor put your trust in prosperity, to set the whole power of fortune before your eyes, and to suppose that she will do what he can do." An evil that hath been long expected gives the milder stroke when it happens.

LUCIUS SENECA, *LETTERS FROM A STOIC*, "LXXVIII. ON SICKNESS, PAIN AND DEATH" (FROM C. 63-65 CE)

ACCEPTANCE

But I congratulate myself with you that, whatever my body may feel, my mind or understanding is not sensible of any decay or injury from time. Vices only are grown old, and whatever is instrumental thereto. The soul still flourisheth and rejoiceth that she hath so little to do with the body. Having partly disrobed herself, she glories in it and makes me even doubt concerning old age. She calls this the flower of age, let us believe her and let her enjoy her proper good. It is a pleasure to me to consider and examine what I owe of this tranquillity, this correctness of morals to wisdom and what to old age, and diligently to enquire what it is I cannot do and what I would not do, and if what I cannot be also what I would not, I have reason to rejoice in my inability. For what cause is there of complaint, what great inconvenience, if what must one day end be now upon the decay?

LUCIUS SENECA, *LETTERS FROM A STOIC*, "XXVII. ON GOOD OLD AGE. MEDITATION ON DEATH" (FROM C. 63-65 CE)

WISDOM

Be not disgusted, nor discouraged, nor dissatisfied, if thou dost not succeed in doing everything according to right principles; but when thou hast failed, return back again, and be content if the greater part of what thou doest is consistent with man's nature, and love this to which thou returnest; and do not return to philosophy as if she were a master… For thus thou wilt not fail to obey reason, and thou wilt repose in it. And remember that philosophy requires only the things which thy nature requires; but thou wouldst have something else which is not according to nature – It may be objected, Why what is more agreeable than this which I am doing? – But is not this the very reason why pleasure deceives us? And consider if magnanimity, freedom, simplicity, equanimity, piety, are not more agreeable. For what is more agreeable than wisdom itself, when thou thinkest of the security and the happy course of all things which depend on the faculty of understanding and knowledge?

MARCUS AURELIUS, *MEDITATIONS*, "BOOK V" (FROM C. 180 CE)

NOBILITY OF THOUGHT

150

Since then it is of necessity that every man uses everything according to the opinion which he has about it, those, the few, who think that they are formed for fidelity and modesty and a sure use of appearances have no mean or ignoble thoughts about themselves; but with the many it is quite the contrary. For they say, What am I? A poor, miserable man, with my wretched bit of flesh. Wretched, indeed; but you possess something better than your bit of flesh. Why then do you neglect that which is better, and why do you attach yourself to this?

EPICTETUS, *THE TEACHINGS OF A STOIC: SELECTED DISCOURSES AND THE ENCHIRIDION*, "HOW A MAN SHOULD PROCEED FROM THE PRINCIPLE OF GOD BEING THE FATHER OF ALL MEN TO THE REST" (FROM C. EARLY 2ND CENTURY CE)

WISDOM

151

Examine men's ruling principles, even those of the wise, what kind of things they avoid, and what kind they pursue.

MARCUS AURELIUS, *MEDITATIONS*, "BOOK IV" (FROM C. 180 CE)

VIRTUE

"Immoderate anger turns to madness." You cannot but know this truth if ever you were master of a stubborn slave or had an enemy. But indeed, this passion is apt to afflict all sorts of persons. It arises as well from love as from hate, it breaks out not only in serious affairs but amidst sport and jesting, nor does it signify so much from what provocation it springs, as what sort of mind it affects, as it is not to be considered how great a fire is but whereon it happens to light. Be it ever so great, it hurts not solid bodies, while such as are dry and combustible soon raise a spark into a mighty flame. Thus it is, Lucilius, the event of an extraordinary passion is madness and therefore anger is to be avoided not only for moderations sake but for the health both of the mind and body.

LUCIUS SENECA, *LETTERS FROM A STOIC*, "XVIII. ON THE BEHAVIOUR OF A PHILOSOPHER AT CERTAIN SEASONS. ON POVERTY AND IMMODERATE ANGER" (FROM C. 63-65 CE)

DETACHMENT

It is peculiar to man to love even those who do wrong. And this happens, if when they do wrong it occurs to thee that they are kinsmen, and that they do wrong through ignorance and unintentionally, and that soon both of you will die; and above all, that the wrongdoer has done thee no harm, for he has not made thy ruling faculty worse than it was before.

MARCUS AURELIUS, *MEDITATIONS*, "BOOK VII" (FROM C. 180 CE)

GOODNESS

But indeed for the power of seeing and hearing, and indeed for life itself, and for the things which contribute to support it, for the fruits which are dry, and for wine and oil give thanks to God: but remember that he has given you something else better than all these, I mean the power of using them, proving them, and estimating the value of each.

EPICTETUS, *THE TEACHINGS OF A STOIC: SELECTED DISCOURSES AND THE ENCHIRIDION*, "ON THE POWER OF SPEAKING" (FROM C. EARLY 2ND CENTURY CE)

ACCEPTANCE

…today I have been reading Epicurus (for you must know I sometimes make an excursion into the enemy's camp, not by way of deserter but as a spy), "cheerful poverty," says he, "is an excellent thing." Now I cannot conceive how that fate can be called poor which is cheerful. The man whose poverty sits easy upon him is rich. Not he that hath little but he that desireth more is the poor man.

LUCIUS SENECA, *LETTERS FROM A STOIC*, "II. ON STUDY, AND TRUE RICHES" (FROM C. 63-65 CE)

WILL

For I force my mind to concentrate, and keep it from straying to things outside itself; all outdoors may be bedlam, provided that there is no disturbance within, provided that fear is not wrangling with desire in my breast, provided that meanness and lavishness are not at odds, one harassing the other. For of what benefit is a quiet neighbourhood, if our emotions are in an uproar?

LUCIUS SENECA, *LETTERS FROM A STOIC*, "LVI. ON TRANQUILLITY" (FROM C. 63-65 CE)

COOPERATION WITH NATURE

…it is a man's duty to comfort himself, and to wait for the natural dissolution and not to be vexed at the delay, but to rest in these principles only: the one, that nothing will happen to me which is not conformable to the nature of the universe; and the other, that it is in my power never to act contrary to my god and daemon: for there is no man who will compel me to this.

MARCUS AURELIUS, *MEDITATIONS*, "BOOK V" (FROM C. 180 CE)

DETACHMENT

[Diogenes] says that death is no evil, for neither is it base; he says that fame (reputation) is the noise of madmen. And what… about pain, about pleasure, and about poverty? He says that to be naked is better than any purple robe, and to sleep on the bare ground is the softest bed; and he gives as a proof of each thing that he affirms his own courage, his tranquillity, his freedom, and the healthy appearance and compactness of his body.
There is no enemy near, he says; all is peace.

EPICTETUS, *THE TEACHINGS OF A STOIC: SELECTED DISCOURSES AND THE ENCHIRIDION*, "HOW WE SHOULD STRUGGLE WITH CIRCUMSTANCES" (FROM C. EARLY 2ND CENTURY CE)

DETACHMENT

For what is weeping and lamenting? Opinion. What is bad fortune? Opinion. What is civil sedition, what is divided opinion, what is blame, what is accusation, what is impiety, what is trifling? All these things are opinions, and nothing more, and opinions about things independent of the will, as if they were good and bad. Let a man transfer these opinions to things dependent on the will, and I engage for him that he will be firm and constant, whatever may be the state of things around him. Such as is a dish of water, such is the soul. Such as is the ray of light which falls on the water, such are the appearances. When the water is moved, the ray also seems to be moved, yet it is not moved. And when then a man is seized with giddiness, it is not the arts and the virtues which are confounded, but the spirit (the nervous power) on which they are impressed; but if the spirit be restored to its settled state, those things also are restored.

EPICTETUS, *THE TEACHINGS OF A STOIC: SELECTED DISCOURSES AND THE ENCHIRIDION*, "WHAT IS THE MATTER ON WHICH A GOOD MAN SHOULD BE EMPLOYED, AND IN WHAT WE OUGHT CHIEFLY TO PRACTISE OURSELVES" (FROM C. EARLY 2ND CENTURY CE)

WISDOM

Add now what belongs to those who are still mere pupils. First, they follow those who have gone before them in that wherein everyone hath dissented from his predecessor. Secondly, they follow them in that which is still to be fought and will never be found if we content ourselves with what is already attained. And lastly, he that follows another invents nothing, nay he seeks nothing. What then? Must I not follow the steps of those who have gone before me? Yes, I will walk in the old path, but if I chance to find one nearer and plainer I shall be inclined to take it and direct others thereto. Truth is open to all men, but as yet hath not been engrossed. Much is left to future generations.

LUCIUS SENECA, *LETTERS FROM A STOIC*, "XXXIII. ON READING AND STUDY. SENTIMENTAL STOICISM" (FROM C. 63-65 CE)

WISDOM

The material for the wise and good man is his own ruling faculty: and the body is the material for the physician and the aliptes (the man who oils persons); the land is the matter for the husbandman. The business of the wise and good man is to use appearances conformably to nature: and as it is the nature of every soul to assent to the truth, to dissent from the false, and to remain in suspense as to that which is uncertain; so it is its nature to be moved towards the desire for the good, and to aversion from the evil; and with respect to that which is neither good nor bad it feels indifferent.

EPICTETUS, *THE TEACHINGS OF A STOIC: SELECTED DISCOURSES AND THE ENCHIRIDION*, "WHAT IS THE MATTER ON WHICH A GOOD MAN SHOULD BE EMPLOYED, AND IN WHAT WE OUGHT CHIEFLY TO PRACTISE OURSELVES" (FROM C. EARLY 2ND CENTURY CE)

CHANGE

Asia, Europe are corners of the universe: all the sea a drop in the universe; Athos a little clod of the universe: all the present time is a point in eternity. All things are little, changeable, perishable.

MARCUS AURELIUS, *MEDITATIONS*, "BOOK VI" (FROM C. 180 CE)

DETACHMENT

And if you see a man, unterrified with danger, untainted with lustful desires, happy in adversity, calm and composed amidst a storm, looking down as from an eminence upon man and on a level with the Gods, seems he not a subject of veneration? Will you not own that you observe something in him, too, great and noble to bear any similitude to the little body of the man that it inhabiteth?

LUCIUS SENECA, *LETTERS FROM A STOIC*, "XLI. THERE IS A CERTAIN DIVINITY IN GOOD MEN" (FROM C. 63-65 CE)

NOBILITY OF THOUGHT

Know you not how small a part you are compared with the whole. I mean with respect to the body, for as to intelligence you are not inferior to the gods nor less; for the magnitude of intelligence is not measured by length nor yet by height, but by thoughts.

EPICTETUS, *THE TEACHINGS OF A STOIC: SELECTED DISCOURSES AND THE ENCHIRIDION*, "OF PROVIDENCE" (FROM C. EARLY 2ND CENTURY CE)

GOODNESS

When the good appears, it immediately attracts to itself; the evil repels from itself. But the soul will never reject the manifest appearance of the good, any more than persons will reject Cæsar's coin. On this principle depends every movement both of man and God.

EPICTETUS, *THE TEACHINGS OF A STOIC: SELECTED DISCOURSES AND THE ENCHIRIDION*, "WHAT IS THE MATTER ON WHICH A GOOD MAN SHOULD BE EMPLOYED, AND IN WHAT WE OUGHT CHIEFLY TO PRACTISE OURSELVES" (FROM C. EARLY 2ND CENTURY CE)

DETACHMENT

Accept the fellowship of poverty. Not that I would debar you from the possession of riches, but would have you so possess them as not to be afraid of losing them. Which intrepid security you may attain by this simple method, only by persuading yourself that you can live happily without them and looking upon them as ever ready to take wing.

LUCIUS SENECA, *LETTERS FROM A STOIC*, "XVIII. ON THE BEHAVIOUR OF A PHILOSOPHER AT CERTAIN SEASONS. ON POVERTY AND IMMODERATE ANGER" (FROM C. 63-65 CE)

GOODNESS

What kind of things those are which appear good to the many, we may learn even from this. For if any man should conceive certain things as being really good, such as prudence, temperance, justice, fortitude, he would not after having first conceived these endure to listen to anything which should not be in harmony with what is really good.

MARCUS AURELIUS, *MEDITATIONS*, "BOOK V" (FROM C. 180 CE)

CHANGE

You think it strange, Lucilius, and as happening to yourself alone that after so long a journey, and the visiting so many different places, you could not throw off your chagrin and melancholy disposition. The mind must be changed for this purpose and not the climate. Though you cross the ocean, though (as our Virgil says), "whitherforever you fly, your vices will still follow."

LUCIUS SENECA, *LETTERS FROM A STOIC*, "XXVIII. CHANGE OF PLACE MAKES NO ALTERATION IN THE MIND" (FROM C. 63-65 CE)

WISDOM

If you have received the impression of any pleasure, guard yourself against being carried away by it; but let the thing wait for you, and allow yourself a certain delay on your own part. Then think of both times, of the time when you will enjoy the pleasure, and of the time after the enjoyment of the pleasure, when you will repent and will reproach yourself. And set against these things how you will rejoice, if you have abstained from the pleasure, and how you will commend yourself. But if it seems to you seasonable to undertake (do) the thing, take care that the charm of it, and the pleasure, and the attraction of it shall not conquer you; but set on the other side the consideration, how much better it is to be conscious that you have gained this victory.

EPICTETUS, *THE TEACHINGS OF A STOIC: SELECTED DISCOURSES AND THE ENCHIRIDION,* "THE MANUAL: XXXIV" (FROM C. EARLY 2ND CENTURY CE)

DETACHMENT

Not that mere water is so pleasant a thing or a coarse cake or a piece of barley bread, but the chief pleasure consists in being able to extract even satisfaction from these and to arrive at such a pass as to bid defiance to the inclemency of fortune. What if the allowance of a common prison is better, and even the executioner supplies the criminals under sentence of death with a larger portion. How great must that mind be to submit to that condition voluntarily that is decreed for those who are reduced to the last extremity! This is to raise, as it were, a counter-battery to Fortune.

LUCIUS SENECA, *LETTERS FROM A STOIC*, "XVIII. ON THE BEHAVIOUR OF A PHILOSOPHER AT CERTAIN SEASONS. ON POVERTY AND IMMODERATE ANGER" (FROM C. 63-65 CE)

ACCEPTANCE

Seek not that the things which happen should happen as you wish; but wish the things which happen to be as they are, and you will have a tranquil flow of life.

EPICTETUS, *THE TEACHINGS OF A STOIC: SELECTED DISCOURSES AND THE ENCHIRIDION*, "THE MANUAL: VIII" (FROM C. EARLY 2ND CENTURY CE)

CHANGE

172

You travel here and there to shake off the inward load, which by such agitation only becomes more troublesome. As in a ship, a burden that is fixed and immoveable strains it the less, while such as are moveable are apt to sink the side to which they roll by their unequal pressure. In everything you do you are still acting against yourself. The very motion cannot but hurt you, it is shaking a sick man.

LUCIUS SENECA, *LETTERS FROM A STOIC*, "XXVIII. CHANGE OF PLACE MAKES NO ALTERATION IN THE MIND" (FROM C. 63-65 CE)

ACCEPTANCE

173

For what avails it, how much a man hath in his chest or in his barns, what stock he has in the field, or what money at interest, if he is still hankering after another's wealth, if he is ever counting not what he has got already but what he may get. Do you ask me what I take to be the proper mean of wealth? I will tell you – first, a supply of necessaries, secondly, an easy competency.

LUCIUS SENECA, *LETTERS FROM A STOIC*, "II. ON STUDY, AND TRUE RICHES" (FROM C. 63-65 CE)

COOPERATION WITH NATURE

So also in man we ought not to value the material, the poor flesh, but the principal (leading) things. What are these? Engaging in public business, marrying, begetting children, venerating God, taking care of parents, and generally, having desires, aversions, pursuits of things and avoidances, in the way in which we ought to do these things, and according to our nature. And how are we constituted by nature? Free, noble, modest; for what other animal blushes? What other is capable of receiving the appearance (the impression) of shame? And we are so constituted by nature as to subject pleasure to these things, as a minister, a servant, in order that it may call forth our activity, in order that it may keep us constant in acts which are conformable to nature.

EPICTETUS, *THE TEACHINGS OF A STOIC: SELECTED DISCOURSES AND THE ENCHIRIDION*, "TO THE ADMINISTRATOR OF THE FREE CITIES WHO WAS AN EPICUREAN" (FROM C. EARLY 2ND CENTURY CE)

CHANGE

…they are upon the continual float and are subject to daily diminution and addition. No one is the same man in old age as he was in youth, no one is the same in the morning that he was yesterday, our bodies are carried away as a river. All that you see runs down with time, nothing still remains the same. Even while I say these things are changed, I am changed myself. This is what Heraclitus means when he says, "we go not twice into the same river. The river still keeps its name but the water passeth away." This indeed is more manifest in a river than in man, but yet as swift a course carries us likewise away and therefore I am surprised at our folly in being fond of so fleeting a thing as is the body and in perpetual fear, lest we should die one day or other when every moment is the death of our former habit of body. And can you be afraid, Lucilius, lest that should happen sometime or other, which happens every day? What I have said relates to man composed of matter, fleeting, frail and subject to variety of accidents. But the world likewise, eternal as it may be and invincible, is still forever changing and remains not the same a moment, for though it may have all things in it it ever had, it possesseth them not in the same manner, the whole order is continually changed.

LUCIUS SENECA, *LETTERS FROM A STOIC*, "LVIII. ON TREATMENT OF SERVANTS" (FROM C. 63-65 CE)

CHANGE

Were you to consider that he whom you call your slave is sprung from the same origin, enjoys the same climate, breathes the same air and is subject to the same condition of life and death, you might as well think it possible for you to see him a gentleman as he to see you a slave. … And can you now despise the man whose fortune is such into which, while you despise it, you may chance to fall?

LUCIUS SENECA, *LETTERS FROM A STOIC*, "XLVII. ON TREATMENT OF SERVANTS" (FROM C. 63-65 CE)

DETACHMENT

It is not possible that what is by nature free can be disturbed by anything else, or hindered by any other thing than by itself. But it is a man's own opinions which disturb him. For when the tyrant says to a man, I will chain your leg, he who values his leg says, Do not; have pity. But he who values his own will says, If it appears more advantageous to you, chain it. Do you not care? I do not care. I will show you that I am master.

EPICTETUS, *THE TEACHINGS OF A STOIC: SELECTED DISCOURSES AND THE ENCHIRIDION*, "HOW WE SHOULD BEHAVE TO TYRANTS" (FROM C. EARLY 2ND CENTURY CE)

NOBILITY OF THOUGHT

In one respect man is the nearest thing to me, so far as I must do good to men and endure them. But so far as some men make themselves obstacles to my proper acts, man becomes to me one of the things which are indifferent, no less than the sun or wind or a wild beast. Now it is true that these may impede my action, but they are no impediments to my affects and disposition, which have the power of acting conditionally and changing: for the mind converts and changes every hindrance to its activity into an aid; and so that which is a hindrance is made a furtherance to an act; and that which is an obstacle on the road helps us on this road.

MARCUS AURELIUS, *MEDITATIONS*, "BOOK V" (FROM C. 180 CE)

GOODNESS

For the ruling principle of a bad man cannot be trusted; it is insecure, has no certain rule by which it is directed, and is overpowered at different times by different appearances.

EPICTETUS, *THE TEACHINGS OF A STOIC: SELECTED DISCOURSES AND THE ENCHIRIDION*, "ON FRIENDSHIP" (FROM C. EARLY 2ND CENTURY CE)

GOODNESS

Yes, a divine power defendeth hither from above, a soul of such excellence and moderation as to look down with a noble scorn on earthly things and so laugh at those tries we are apt to wish for or fear cannot but be enkindled by the deity within, so great a quality cannot subsist but by the help of God. He is there in part, though still remaining above in the Heavens. As the rays of the sun reach, and with their influence pierce the Earth, and yet are still above in the body from whence they proceed, so a mind, great and holy, and thus humbled to give us a more adequate knowledge of divine things dwells indeed with us, but still adheres to its original. It depends upon that, thither tend all its views and pious endeavours vastly superior to, however concerned in, human affairs.

LUCIUS SENECA, *LETTERS FROM A STOIC*, "XLI. THERE IS A CERTAIN DIVINITY IN GOOD MEN" (FROM C. 63-65 CE)

DETACHMENT

"Confide whether it be better, that Death should come to us or we go to him." The sense is plain. It is an excellent thing to know what Death is and how to die. You perhaps may think it unnecessary to learn that which can but once be of any use. Now this is the very reason why we ought to study it. We must always be learning that which we never can be assured we rightly know. Think upon Death. He that commands this bids you think upon liberty. He that hath learned to die hath unlearned to be a slave. Death is above every power upon Earth, at least beyond it. What is a prison, or guards, or bars to him? The passage is still free and open, but there is a strong chain, which still binds us down, the love of life, which as it is not to be thrown off at once, may yet be eased and lessened that, when an exigency requires, nothing may detain or hinder us from being prepared and ready to submit to that which we must one day certainly undergo.

LUCIUS SENECA, *LETTERS FROM A STOIC*, "XII. ON GOOD OLD AGE. MEDITATION ON DEATH" (FROM C. 63-65 CE)

GOODNESS

Reverence that which is best in the universe; and this is that which makes use of all things and directs all things. And in like manner also reverence that which is best in thyself; and this is of the same kind as that. For in thyself also, that which makes use of everything else, is this, and thy life is directed by this.

MARCUS AURELIUS, *MEDITATIONS*, "BOOK V" (FROM C. 180 CE)

VIRTUE

"The acknowledgement of a crime is the first step to reformation." This is an excellent saying from Epicurus, for he that knows not when he trespasseth can never desire to be reformed. You must accuse yourself before you can mend. There are some who even glory in their sins, and do you think they will ever be solicitous for a remedy who account their vices as so many virtues? As much as possible, therefore, reprove yourself, examine yourself thoroughly first so the office of an informer, then of a judge and lastly of an intercessor, though a little wholesome punishment may be sometimes not amiss.

LUCIUS SENECA, *LETTERS FROM A STOIC*, "XXVIII. CHANGE OF PLACE MAKES NO ALTERATION IN THE MIND" (FROM C. 63-65 CE)

WILL

But what is philosophizing? Is it not a preparation against events which may happen?… If we give up philosophy, what shall we gain? What then should a man say on the occasion of each painful thing? It was for this that I exercised myself, for this I disciplined myself. God says to you: Give me a proof that you have duly practised athletics, that you have eaten what you ought, that you have been exercised… Then do you show yourself weak when the time for action comes? Now is the time for the fever. Let it be borne well. Now is the time for thirst, bear it well. Now is the time for hunger, bear it well. Is it not in your power? Who shall hinder you? The physician will hinder you from drinking; but he cannot prevent you from bearing thirst well: and he will hinder you from eating; but he cannot prevent you from bearing hunger well.

EPICTETUS, *THE TEACHINGS OF A STOIC: SELECTED DISCOURSES AND THE ENCHIRIDION*, "IN WHAT MANNER WE OUGHT TO BEAR SICKNESS" (FROM C. EARLY 2ND CENTURY CE)

VIRTUE

Number your years, Seneca, and you will be ashamed to desire and be hunting after those things wherein you delighted when a child. And be it your particular care on this side the grave that your vices may all die before you. Forego those turbulent and dear-bought pleasures that hurt, not only before but after enjoyment, as crimes though not found out when perpetrated still carry anxiety with them. All unlawful pleasures are attended with remorse, there is no solidity in them nor anything worthy of confidence, even though they hurt not they soon pass and are gone. Look out rather for something more substantial and lasting. But alas! There is no such thing, except what the mind can find within itself, virtue only can give perpetual joy and security. Whatever may seem to obstruct it passeth over like a cloud, which for a moment darkens but cannot hide the day. ... You have not indeed been idle, Seneca, but this is not enough, you must still exert yourself, a great deal remains to be done.

LUCIUS SENECA, *LETTERS FROM A STOIC*, "XXVII. VIRTUE ONLY IS SECURE" (FROM C. 63–65 CE)

TIME

Often think of the rapidity with which things pass by and disappear, both the things which are and the things which are produced. For substance is like a river in a continual flow, and the activities of things are in constant change, and the causes work in infinite varieties; and there is hardly anything which stands still. And consider this which is near to thee, this boundless abyss of the past and of the future in which all things disappear. How then is he not a fool who is puffed up with such things or plagued about them and makes himself miserable? For they vex him only for a time, and a short time. Think of the universal substance, of which thou hast a very small portion; and of universal time, of which a short and indivisible interval has been assigned to thee; and of that which is fixed by destiny, and how small a part of it thou art.

MARCUS AURELIUS, *MEDITATIONS*, "BOOK V" (FROM C. 180 CE)

VIRTUE

"Is he a slave?" His mind may yet be free. "Is he a slave?" Why should this prejudice you against him? Show me the man who is not a slave. One is a slave to lust, another to covetousness, another to ambition, and all to fear. I can show you a man of consular dignity, a slave to an old woman, a very rich man a slave to his handmaid, and many a young nobleman who are the very bond-slaves of players. No slavery is more infamous than that which is voluntary.

LUCIUS SENECA, *LETTERS FROM A STOIC*, "XLVII. ON TREATMENT OF SERVANTS" (FROM C. 63-65 CE)

CHANGE

…let us not dread injuries, or wounds, or chains, or poverty, or death itself. For what is death? It is either an end of life or the passage into another and why should I fear to be no more, since that is the same as not to have been? Much less I have reason to be afraid of passing elsewhere, for wherever I go I shall certainly be more at large than I am at present.

LUCIUS SENECA, *LETTERS FROM A STOIC*, "LXV. ON THE FIRST CAUSE" (FROM C. 63-65 CE)

COOPERATION WITH NATURE

But I cannot attend to my philosophical studies. And for what purpose do you follow them? Slave, is it not that you may be happy, that you may be constant, is it not that you may be in a state conformable to nature and live so? What hinders you when you have a fever from having your ruling faculty conformable to nature? Here is the proof of the thing, here is the test of the philosopher… What is it to bear a fever well? Not to blame God or man; not to be afflicted at that which happens, to expect death well and nobly, to do what must be done…

EPICTETUS, *THE TEACHINGS OF A STOIC: SELECTED DISCOURSES AND THE ENCHIRIDION*, "IN WHAT MANNER WE OUGHT TO BEAR SICKNESS" (FROM C. EARLY 2ND CENTURY CE)

DETACHMENT

Return to thy sober senses and call thyself back; and when thou hast roused thyself from sleep and hast perceived that they were only dreams which troubled thee, now in thy waking hours look at these [the things about thee] as thou didst look at those [the dreams].

MARCUS AURELIUS, *MEDITATIONS*, "BOOK VI" (FROM C. 180 CE)

WILL

Theophrastus, in his comparison of bad acts – such a comparison as one would make in accordance with the common notions of mankind – says, like a true philosopher, that the offences which are committed through desire are more blameable than those which are committed through anger. For he who is excited by anger seems to turn away from reason with a certain pain and unconscious contraction; but he who offends through desire, being overpowered by pleasure, seems to be in a manner more intemperate… in his offences. Rightly then, and in a way worthy of philosophy, he said that the offence which is committed with pleasure is more blameable than that which is committed with pain; and on the whole the one is more like a person who has been first wronged and through pain is compelled to be angry; but the other is moved by his own impulse to do wrong, being carried towards doing something by desire.

MARCUS AURELIUS, *MEDITATIONS*, "BOOK II" (FROM C. 180 CE)

DETACHMENT

For they do not understand how a man passes his life when he is alone, because they set out from a certain natural principle, from the natural desire of community and mutual love and from the pleasure of conversation among men. But nonetheless a man ought to be prepared in a manner for this also (being alone), to be able to be sufficient for himself and to be his own companion. For as Zeus dwells with himself, and is tranquil by himself, and thinks of his own administration and of its nature, and is employed in thoughts suitable to himself; so ought we also to be able to talk with ourselves, not to feel the want of others also, not to be unprovided with the means of passing our time; to observe the divine administration, and the relation of ourselves to everything else; to consider how we formerly were affected towards things that happened and how at present; what are still the things which give us pain; how these also can be cured and how removed; if any things require improvement, to improve them according to reason.

EPICTETUS, *THE TEACHINGS OF A STOIC: SELECTED DISCOURSES AND THE ENCHIRIDION*, "WHAT SOLITUDE IS, AND WHAT KIND OF PERSON A SOLITARY MAN IS" (FROM C. EARLY 2ND CENTURY CE)

WISDOM

He gives a sure token of his steadiness who is not to be drawn into softness and luxury at such a time, and so much stronger is he if he keeps himself sober and thirsty when all the people are drunk and overcharged. But the more moderate way is not to be particular at this time so as to be taken notice of, nor yet to give into all their measures, but to do what others do, though not in the same manner. A man may celebrate a festival without luxury and excess of riot.

LUCIUS SENECA, *LETTERS FROM A STOIC*, "XVIII. ON THE BEHAVIOUR OF A PHILOSOPHER AT CERTAIN SEASONS. ON POVERTY AND IMMODERATE ANGER" (FROM C. 63-65 CE)

DETACHMENT

If then you desire (aim at) such great things remember that you must not (attempt to) lay hold of them with a small effort; but you must leave alone some things entirely, and postpone others for the present.

EPICTETUS, *THE TEACHINGS OF A STOIC: SELECTED DISCOURSES AND THE ENCHIRIDION*, "THE MANUAL: I" (FROM C. EARLY 2ND CENTURY CE)

DETACHMENT

Let the part of thy soul which leads and governs be undisturbed by the movements in the flesh, whether of pleasure or of pain; and let it not unite with them, but let it circumscribe itself and limit those affects to their parts. But when these affects rise up to the mind by virtue of that other sympathy that naturally exists in a body which is all one, then thou must not strive to resist the sensation, for it is natural: but let not the ruling part of itself add to the sensation the opinion that it is either good or bad.

MARCUS AURELIUS, *MEDITATIONS*, "BOOK V" (FROM C. 180 CE)

VIRTUE

…we must cautiously enter into such intimacies with those of the common sort, and remember that it is impossible that a man can keep company with one who is covered with soot without being partaker of the soot himself.

EPICTETUS, *THE TEACHINGS OF A STOIC: SELECTED DISCOURSES AND THE ENCHIRIDION*, "THAT WE OUGHT WITH CAUTION TO ENTER INTO FAMILIAR INTERCOURSE WITH MEN" (FROM C. EARLY 2ND CENTURY CE)

GOODNESS

Solitude is a certain condition of a helpless man. For because a man is alone, he is not for that reason also solitary; just as though a man is among numbers, he is not therefore not solitary. When then we have lost either a brother, or a son, or a friend on whom we were accustomed to repose, we say that we are left solitary, though we are often in Rome, though such a crowd meet us, though so many live in the same place… For the man who is solitary, as it is conceived, is considered to be a helpless person and exposed to those who wish to harm him. For this reason when we travel, then especially do we say that we are lonely when we fall among robbers, for it is not the sight of a human creature which removes us from solitude, but the sight of one who is faithful and modest and helpful to us…

EPICTETUS, *THE TEACHINGS OF A STOIC: SELECTED DISCOURSES AND THE ENCHIRIDION*, "WHAT SOLITUDE IS, AND WHAT KIND OF PERSON A SOLITARY MAN IS" (FROM C. EARLY 2ND CENTURY CE)

VIRTUE

It matters not where you come but what sort of man you come thither. The mind is not to be devoted to any particular place. We must live in the world under this persuasion. "I am not born for one corner of it more than another, the whole is my native country." Was this manifest to you, you would be no longer surprised at not finding any benefit from the difference of place when weary of one you fly to another. For the first would have pleased you if you had thought it your own. You do not travel but wander, and are driven about from place to place, whereas what you are in search of, a good life, is to be found anywhere.

LUCIUS SENECA, *LETTERS FROM A STOIC*, "XXVIII. CHANGE OF PLACE MAKES NO ALTERATION IN THE MIND" (FROM C. 63–65 CE)

CHANGE

Nature which governs the whole will soon change all things which thou seest, and out of their substance will make other things, and again other things from the substance of them…

MARCUS AURELIUS, *MEDITATIONS*, "BOOK VII" (FROM C. 180 CE)

GOODNESS

Art thou angry with him whose armpits stink? Art thou angry with him whose mouth smells foul? What good will this danger do thee? He has such a mouth, he has such armpits: it is necessary that such an emanation must come from such things – but the man has reason, it will be said, and he is able, if he takes pain, to discover wherein he offends – I wish thee well of thy discovery. Well then, and thou hast reason: by thy rational faculty stir up his rational faculty; show him his error, admonish him. For if he listens, thou wilt cure him, and there is no need of anger.

MARCUS AURELIUS, *MEDITATIONS*, "BOOK V" (FROM C. 180 CE)

WILL

Death is a cessation of the impressions through the senses, and of the pulling of the strings which move the appetites, and of the discursive movements of the thoughts, and of the service to the flesh. It is a shame for the soul to be first to give way in this life, when thy body does not give way.

MARCUS AURELIUS, *MEDITATIONS*, "BOOK VI" (FROM C. 180 CE)

GOODNESS

…he can bear the loss of a friend patiently, though perhaps he will not be long without one, as it is in his power to repair the loss when he pleases. … You may ask, perhaps, what method a man must take so soon to gain a friend? … Hecaton [says], "I will disclose to you an excellent philtre, without the use of love-powder, herb or bewitching charm – love, that you may be beloved." Now there is a pleasure, not only in the habit of a sure and lasting friendship, but also in the acquisition and beginning of a new one. … Attalus the philosopher was wont to say, "there is more pleasure in making a friend than in having one."

LUCIUS SENECA, *LETTERS FROM A STOIC*, "IX. ON FRIENDSHIP, SELF-COMPLACENCY AND CONTENTMENT" (FROM C. 63-65 CE)

GOODNESS

Whatever anyone does or says, I must be good, just as if the gold, or the emerald, or the purple were always saying this. I must be emerald and keep my colour.

MARCUS AURELIUS, *MEDITATIONS*, "BOOK VII" (FROM C. 180 CE)

COOPERATION WITH NATURE

The desires of nature have their limits, but those that arise from false opinion have nowhere to rest, for they know no bounds. He that walks in a straight and beaten path will soon find an end, but he that wanders out of his way will long wander for error is infinite. Withdraw yourself therefore from vain superfluities … from a natural or a fond and blind desire, consider whether such a thing, if obtained, can give you solid contentment, if not, if as far as you have gone you must still go further, you may be assured that the path you walk in is not the right path of nature.

LUCIUS SENECA, *LETTERS FROM A STOIC*, "XVI. ON THE STUDY OF PHILOSOPHY" (FROM C. 63-65 CE)

COOPERATION WITH NATURE

Always run to the short way; and the short way is the natural: accordingly say and do everything in conformity with the soundest reason. For such a purpose frees a man from trouble, and warfare, and all artifice and ostentatious display.

MARCUS AURELIUS, *MEDITATIONS*, "BOOK IV" (FROM C. 180 CE)

ACCEPTANCE

If you bear a fever well, you have all that belongs to a man in a fever. What is it to bear a fever well? Not to blame God or man; not to be afflicted at that which happens, to expect death well and nobly, to do what must be done: when the physician comes in, not to be frightened at what he says; nor if he says you are doing well, to be overjoyed. For what good has he told you? And when you were in health, what good was that to you? And even if he says you are in a bad way, do not despond. For what is it to be ill? Is it that you are near the severance of the soul and the body? What harm is there in this? If you are not near now, will you not afterwards be near? Is the world going to be turned upside down when you are dead?

EPICTETUS, *THE TEACHINGS OF A STOIC: SELECTED DISCOURSES AND THE ENCHIRIDION*, "IN WHAT MANNER WE OUGHT TO BEAR SICKNESS" (FROM C. EARLY 2ND CENTURY CE)

VIRTUE

And call to recollection both how many things thou hast passed through, and how many things thou hast been able to endure: and that the history of thy life is now complete and thy service is ended: and how many beautiful things thou hast seen: and how many pleasures and pains thou hast despised; and how many things called honourable thou hast spurned; and to how many ill-minded folks thou hast shown a kind disposition.

MARCUS AURELIUS, *MEDITATIONS*, "BOOK V" (FROM C. 180 CE)

CHANGE

Every great power (faculty) is dangerous to beginners. You must then bear such things as you are able, but conformably to nature… Practise sometimes a way of living like a person out of health that you may at some time live like a man in health.

EPICTETUS, *THE TEACHINGS OF A STOIC: SELECTED DISCOURSES AND THE ENCHIRIDION*, "WHAT SOLITUDE IS, AND WHAT KIND OF PERSON A SOLITARY MAN IS" (FROM C. EARLY 2ND CENTURY CE)

CHANGE

As bad tragic actors cannot sing alone, but in company with many, so some persons cannot walk about alone. Man, if you are anything, both walk alone and talk to yourself, and do not hide yourself in the chorus. Examine a little at last, look around, stir yourself up, that you may know who you are.

EPICTETUS, *THE TEACHINGS OF A STOIC: SELECTED DISCOURSES AND THE ENCHIRIDION*, "WHAT SOLITUDE IS, AND WHAT KIND OF PERSON A SOLITARY MAN IS" (FROM C. EARLY 2ND CENTURY CE)

NOBILITY OF THOUGHT

But in truth it is not the place, be it where it will, that can confer true tranquillity, it is the mind that is all in all. I have seen chagrin and melancholy in the most pleasant and cheerful villa, and I have seen men in the midst of solitude fatigued, as it were, with business. There is no reason, therefore, you should complain of your situation because you are not in Campania.

LUCIUS SENECA, *LETTERS FROM A STOIC*, "LV. A TRUE FRIEND IS NEVER ABSENT" (FROM C. 63-65 CE)

VIRTUE

You must root out of men these two things, arrogance (pride) and distrust. Arrogance then is the opinion that you want nothing (are deficient in nothing); but distrust is the opinion that you cannot be happy when so many circumstances surround you. Arrogance is removed by confutation; and Socrates was the first who practised this. And (to know) that the thing is not impossible inquire and seek. This search will do you no harm; and in a manner this is philosophizing, to seek how it is possible to employ desire and aversion without impediment.

EPICTETUS, *THE TEACHINGS OF A STOIC: SELECTED DISCOURSES AND THE ENCHIRIDION*, "CERTAIN MISCELLANEOUS MATTERS" (FROM C. EARLY 2ND CENTURY CE)

CHANGE

Canst thou be nourished, unless the food undergoes a change? ... Dost thou not see then that for thyself also to change is just the same, and equally necessary for the universal nature?

MARCUS AURELIUS, *MEDITATIONS*, "BOOK VII" (FROM C. 180 CE)

GOODNESS

…what is expedient for me is also expedient for you; or I am not your friend if what concerns you is not of like concern to me. Friendship makes a mutual interchange of things necessary, be it either in prosperity or adversity. True friends have all things in common, nor can anyone live happily who lives to himself alone and confides nothing further than his own advantage. You must live for others if you would live honourably for yourself. This social virtue is to be diligently and religiously observed, which blends us all one with another and points out one common right to mankind, but has most efficacy in cultivating the interior society of friendship. For he will certainly have all things in common with a friend, who knows that he hath many things in common with man, his fellow-creature.

LUCIUS SENECA, *LETTERS FROM A STOIC*, "XLVIII. ON SOCIAL VIRTUE AND THE TRIFLING OF SOPHISTRY" (FROM C. 63-65 CE)

NOBILITY OF THOUGHT

This is the true athlete, the man who exercises himself against such appearances… Great is the combat, divine is the work; it is for kingship, for freedom, for happiness, for freedom from perturbation. Remember God; call on him as a helper and protector, as men at sea call on the Dioscuri in a storm. For what is a greater storm than that which comes from appearances which are violent and drive away the reason? For the storm itself, what else is it but an appearance? For take away the fear of death, and suppose as many thunders and lightnings as you please, and you will know what calm and serenity there is in the ruling faculty.

EPICTETUS, *THE TEACHINGS OF A STOIC: SELECTED DISCOURSES AND THE ENCHIRIDION*, "HOW WE SHOULD STRUGGLE AGAINST APPEARANCES" (FROM C. EARLY 2ND CENTURY CE)

ACCEPTANCE

Why then dost thou not wait in tranquility for thy end, whether it is extinction or removal to another state? And until that time comes, what is sufficient? Why, what else than to venerate the gods and bless them, and to do good to men, and to practise tolerance and self-restraint; but as to everything which is beyond the limits of the poor flesh and breath, to remember that this is neither thine nor in thy power. Thou canst pass thy life in an equable flow of happiness, if thou canst go by the right way, and think and act in the right way. These two things are common both to the soul of God and to the soul of man, and to the soul of every rational being, not to be hindered by another; and to hold good to consist in the disposition to justice and the practice of it, and in this to let thy desire find its termination.

MARCUS AURELIUS, *MEDITATIONS*, "BOOK V" (FROM C. 180 CE)

COOPERATION WITH NATURE

…on every side they all stretch out their hands to you and implore your assistance with regard to the life that is past and is still decaying. In you is all their hope and strength, they beseech you to deliver them from this storm of trouble and vexation and show the clear light of truth to such as are distracted with error. Distinguish to them what Nature hath made necessary from what is vain and superfluous, what easy laws she hath imposed upon mankind, how pleasant life may be made, how free and easy to such as follow her laws and how severe and intricate to those who rather trust to opinion than nature.

LUCIUS SENECA, *LETTERS FROM A STOIC*, "XLVIII. ON SOCIAL VIRTUE AND THE TRIFLING OF SOPHISTRY" (FROM C. 63-65 CE)

WISDOM

…restlessness which generally springs from some malady in the mind. The chief testimony, I apprehend, of a mind truly calm and composed is that it is consistent with and can enjoy itself.

LUCIUS SENECA, *LETTERS FROM A STOIC*, "II. ON STUDY, AND TRUE RICHES" (FROM C. 63-65 CE)

COOPERATION WITH NATURE

…as that saying of Epicurus, "if you live according to Nature you will never be poor, if according to opinion, never rich. What Nature demands is little, what opinion, immense." Let the possessions of many rich men be heaped upon you, let fortune exalt you far above any private condition of life, let her cover you with a roof of gold, clothe you with purple, surround you with delicacies and so enrich you as to have the ground whereon you walk paved with marble and bestow upon you not only money enough for use, but to squander away. Add to these statues, pictures and whatever else art can supply the most luxurious fancy with, the issue of all will be only an inducement, still to covet something more.

LUCIUS SENECA, *LETTERS FROM A STOIC*, "XVI. ON THE STUDY OF PHILOSOPHY" (FROM C. 63-65 CE)

TIME

Plain and simple arguments best become and set forth truth. Even had we more time in life it must be sparingly laid out that we might have enough for necessaries. But now what madness is it to learn trifles when life is so very short?

LUCIUS SENECA, *LETTERS FROM A STOIC*, "XLVIII. ON SOCIAL VIRTUE AND THE TRIFLING OF SOPHISTRY" (FROM C. 63-65 CE)

DETACHMENT

These reasonings do not cohere: I am richer than you, therefore I am better than you; I am more eloquent than you, therefore I am better than you. On the contrary, these rather cohere: I am richer than you, therefore my possessions are greater than yours; I am more eloquent than you, therefore my speech is superior to yours. But you are neither possession nor speech.

EPICTETUS, *THE TEACHINGS OF A STOIC: SELECTED DISCOURSES AND THE ENCHIRIDION*, "THE MANUAL: XLII" (FROM C. EARLY 2ND CENTURY CE)

ACCEPTANCE

You should come to him and say: Epictetus, we can no longer endure being bound to this poor body, and feeding it, and giving it drink and rest, and cleaning it, and for the sake of the body complying with the wishes of these and of those. Are not these things indifferent and nothing to us; and is not death no evil? And are we not in a manner kinsmen of God, and did we not come from him? Allow us to depart to the place from which we came; allow us to be released at last from these bonds by which we are bound and weighed down... And I on my part would say: Friends, wait for God: when he shall give the signal and release you from this service, then go to him; but for the present endure to dwell in this place where he has put you. Short indeed is this time of your dwelling here, and easy to bear for those who are so disposed; for what tyrant, or what thief, or what courts of justice are formidable to those who have thus considered as things of no value the body and the possessions of the body? Wait then, do not depart without a reason.

EPICTETUS, *THE TEACHINGS OF A STOIC: SELECTED DISCOURSES AND THE ENCHIRIDION,* "HOW FROM THE FACT THAT WE ARE AKIN TO GOD A MAN MAY PROCEED TO THE CONSEQUENCES" (FROM C. EARLY 2ND CENTURY CE)

COOPERATION WITH NATURE

If a man should be able to assent to this doctrine as he ought, that we are all sprung from God in an especial manner, and that God is the father both of men and of gods, I suppose that he would never have any ignoble or mean thoughts about himself… Yet we do not so; but since these two things are mingled in the generation of man, body in common with the animals, and reason and intelligence in common with the gods, many incline to this kinship, which is miserable and mortal; and some few to that which is divine and happy.

EPICTETUS, *THE TEACHINGS OF A STOIC: SELECTED DISCOURSES AND THE ENCHIRIDION*, "HOW A MAN SHOULD PROCEED FROM THE PRINCIPLE OF GOD BEING THE FATHER OF ALL MEN TO THE REST" (FROM C. EARLY 2ND CENTURY CE)

TIME

Everything material soon disappears in the substance of the whole; and everything formal [causal] is very soon taken back into the universal reason; and the memory of everything is very soon overwhelmed in time.

MARCUS AURELIUS, *MEDITATIONS*, "BOOK VII" (FROM C. 180 CE)

COOPERATION WITH NATURE

The substance of the universe is obedient and compliant; and the reason which governs it has in itself no cause for doing evil, for it has no malice, nor does it do evil to anything, nor is anything harmed by it. But all things are made and perfected according to this reason.

MARCUS AURELIUS, *MEDITATIONS*, "BOOK VI" (FROM C. 180 CE)

CHANGE

Perhaps you will say it is the greatest inconvenience imaginable to be infirm, to languish or, to speak properly, to be melted down. For we are not forcibly laid low on a sudden, we gradually waste away, every day purloins something from our strength. And what exit can be happier than to be dissolved, as it were, by a gentle decay of nature? Not that there is anything very grievous in a stroke or sudden departure out of life, but because it is easy and natural thus to steal away by degrees.

LUCIUS SENECA, *LETTERS FROM A STOIC*, "XII. ON GOOD OLD AGE. MEDITATION ON DEATH" (FROM C. 63-65 CE)

NOBILITY OF THOUGHT

Men are disturbed not by the things which happen, but by the opinions about the things; for example, death is nothing terrible, for if it were it would have seemed so to Socrates; for the opinion about death that it is terrible, is the terrible thing. When then we are impeded, or disturbed, or grieved, let us never blame others, but ourselves – that is, our opinions. It is the act of an ill-instructed man to blame others for his own bad condition; it is the act of one who has begun to be instructed, to lay the blame on himself; and of one whose instruction is completed, neither to blame another, nor himself.

EPICTETUS, *THE TEACHINGS OF A STOIC: SELECTED DISCOURSES AND THE ENCHIRIDION*, "THE MANUAL: V" (FROM C. EARLY 2ND CENTURY CE)

VIRTUE

Thou wilt soon die, and thou art not yet simple, not free from perturbations, nor without suspicion of being hurt by external things, nor kindly disposed towards all; nor dost thou yet place wisdom only in acting justly.

MARCUS AURELIUS, *MEDITATIONS*, "BOOK IV" (FROM C. 180 CE)

WISDOM

Presume not too soon and easily on your own strength, examine well yourself, make different scrutinies and observations, but more especially consider this, whether you have made a progress in philosophy or in life itself, in knowledge or in practice. Philosophy is no popular artifice, nor made for show and ostentation. It consists not in words but in deeds. Nor is it to be applied to only as an amusement, to take off the tediousness of the day. No, it forms and fashions the mind, sets life in good order, directs the conduct, shows what is to be done and what to be left undone, it sits at the helm and steers our course through the wide sea of doubt. In short, no man can live in safety without it. Innumerable accidents happen every hour, which must have recourse to philosophy as a faithful counsellor.

LUCIUS SENECA, *LETTERS FROM A STOIC*, "XVI. ON THE STUDY OF PHILOSOPHY" (FROM C. 63-65 CE)

DETACHMENT

He who has a vehement desire for posthumous fame does not consider that every one of those who remember him will himself also die very soon; then again also they who have succeeded them, until the whole remembrance shall have been extinguished as it is transmitted through men who foolishly admire and perish. But suppose that those who will remember are even immortal, and that the remembrance will be immortal, what then is this to thee? And I say not what is it to the dead, but what is it to the living? What is praise except indeed so far as it has a certain utility? For thou now rejectest unseasonably the gift of nature, clinging to something else…

MARCUS AURELIUS, *MEDITATIONS*, "BOOK IV" (FROM C. 180 CE)

COOPERATION WITH NATURE

Everything harmonizes with me, which is harmonious to thee, O Universe. Nothing for me is too early nor too late, which is in due time for thee. Everything is fruit to me which thy seasons bring, O Nature: from thee are all things, in thee are all things, to thee all things return.

MARCUS AURELIUS, *MEDITATIONS*, "BOOK IV" (FROM C. 180 CE)

CHANGE

I am composed of the formal and the material; and neither of them will perish into nonexistence, as neither of them came into existence out of nonexistence. Every part of me then will be reduced by change into some part of the universe, and that again will change into another part of the universe, and so on forever. And by consequence of such a change I too exist, and those who begot me, and so on forever in the other direction.

MARCUS AURELIUS, *MEDITATIONS*, "BOOK V" (FROM C. 180 CE)

COOPERATION WITH NATURE

In the morning when thou risest unwillingly, let this thought be present – I am rising to the work of a human being. Why then am I dissatisfied if I am going to do the things for which I exist and for which I was brought into the world? Or have I been made for this, to lie in the bedclothes and keep myself warm? But this is more pleasant. Dost thou exist then to take thy pleasure, and not at all for action or exertion?

MARCUS AURELIUS, *MEDITATIONS*, "BOOK V" (FROM C. 180 CE)

CHANGE

...as the flame cannot be suppressed but still flies round that which would press it down, and as the air is not hurt by any stroke you give it, nor indeed divided, but that by its elasticity it pours back again upon the place it has quitted. So the soul, which is of the finest and most subtle quality, cannot be surprised and crushed within the body but by reason of its subtlety breaks forth from whatever seems to overwhelm it. As the lightning, having darted its influence far and wide, returns through a small crevice, so the soul which is far more subtle than flame takes its flight through every pore of the body. From whence ariseth a question concerning immortality, and this you may be assured of, Lucilius, that if it survives the body it can by no means perish because it is not perishable, since no immortality admits an exception, nor can anything destroy what is naturally eternal.

LUCIUS SENECA, *LETTERS FROM A STOIC*, "LVII. ON FEAR AND THE IMMORTALITY OF THE SOUL" (FROM C. 63-65 CE)

NOBILITY OF THOUGHT

Do you ask in what the difference between you shall consist? They will continue longer. But it is the glory of a skilful artist to include much in a little compass. The few days of a wise man are as much to him as his eternity is to God. Nay, there is something wherein the wise man has the advantage of the gods themselves, they are what they are by nature, the wise man is what he is by his own industry. Behold, a wonderful thing to have the weakness of a man and the security of God. Incredible is the strength of philosophy in repelling every violent attack from without, not one of fortune's darts can fix itself in her, she is everywhere guarded and impenetrable.

LUCIUS SENECA, *LETTERS FROM A STOIC*, "LIII. THE GREAT POWER AND VALUE OF PHILOSOPHY" (FROM C. 63-65 CE)

COOPERATION WITH NATURE

Consider thyself to be dead, and to have completed thy life up to the present time; and live according to nature the remainder which is allowed thee.

MARCUS AURELIUS, *MEDITATIONS*, "BOOK VII" (FROM C. 180 CE)

GOODNESS

Try how the life of the good man suits thee, the life of him who is satisfied with his portion out of the whole, and satisfied with his own just acts and benevolent disposition. Hast thou seen those things? Look also at these. Do not disturb thyself. Make thyself all simplicity. Does anyone do wrong? It is to himself that he does the wrong. Has anything happened to thee? Well; out of the universe from the beginning everything which happens has been apportioned and spun out to thee. In a word, thy life is short. Thou must turn to profit the present by the aid of reason and justice. Be sober in thy relaxation. Either it is a well-arranged universe or a chaos huddled together, but still a universe. But can a certain order subsist in thee, and disorder in the All?

MARCUS AURELIUS, *MEDITATIONS*, "BOOK IV" (FROM C. 180 CE)

ACCEPTANCE

Now this is the difference between us (Stoics) and them (the Epicureans). Our wise man gets the better of every evil but yet he feels it, whereas their wise man pretends not to feel it. In this, however, we agree, a wise man is contented and satisfied in himself, and yet, as sufficient as he is in himself, according to our tenets he desires to have a friend, a neighbour, a companion. And as to the contentment we are speaking of, he is contented with a part, as it were, of himself. For should he have lost a hand by any disease or by the sword of an enemy, or suppose by some accident an eye, he is contented with that which is left and will live as cheerfully with his maimed body as if it were entire. What is wanting he will not sigh for in vain, though at the same time, no doubt, he had rather not want it. And thus is a wise man satisfied in himself, not that he desires to have no friend but he knows how to be content without one.

LUCIUS SENECA, *LETTERS FROM A STOIC*, "IX. ON FRIENDSHIP, SELF-COMPLACENCY AND CONTENTMENT" (FROM C. 63–65 CE)

DETACHMENT

As on a voyage when the vessel has reached a port, if you go out to get water it is an amusement by the way to pick up a shellfish or some bulb, but your thoughts ought to be directed to the ship, and you ought to be constantly watching if the captain should call, and then you must throw away all those things, that you may not be bound and pitched into the ship like sheep. So in life also, if there be given to you instead of a little bulb and a shell a wife and child, there will be nothing to prevent (you from taking them). But if the captain should call, run to the ship and leave all those things without regard to them. But if you are old, do not even go far from the ship, lest when you are called you make default.

EPICTETUS, *THE TEACHINGS OF A STOIC: SELECTED DISCOURSES AND THE ENCHIRIDION*, "THE MANUAL: VII" (FROM C. EARLY 2ND CENTURY CE)

GOODNESS

To what purpose then have I chosen a friend? Why to have one whom I would serve to the utmost in case of necessity would follow him into banishment, and for whose life and preservation I would expose myself to danger and death. What you are pleased to call friendship is not friendship but mere traffick, having regard only to some advantage that may accrue there from. No doubt the affection of lovers hath something in it very like friendship, but it is still imperfect and may be called a sort of insane friendship. Is it then founded on the views of profit, of ambition, or of glory? No, love of its own pure motive, neglectful of all other considerations, incites the mind to the desire of beauty not without hopes of mutual endearments. And what then? Does a vile affection spring from or form an alliance upon a more honourable cause? But this, you say, is not the point in question whether friendship is desirable merely upon its own account, for if so the man who is satisfied in himself may well accede thereto as to the most lovely object, not allured by any hope of gain or disheartened at any change of fortune. He detracts from the majesty of friendship who enters upon it merely as a preservative against evil accidents.

LUCIUS SENECA, *LETTERS FROM A STOIC*, "IX. ON FRIENDSHIP, SELF-COMPLACENCY AND CONTENTMENT" (FROM C. 63-65 CE)

WISDOM

Pleasure... Subject it to the rule, throw it into the balance. Ought the good to be such a thing that it is fit that we have confidence in it? Yes. And in which we ought to confide? It ought to be. Is it fit to trust to anything which is insecure? No. Is then pleasure anything secure? No. Take it then and throw it out of the scale, and drive it far away from the place of good things. But if you are not sharp sighted, and one balance is not enough for you, bring another. Is it fit to be elated over what is good? Yes. Is it proper then to be elated over present pleasure? ... Thus things are tested and weighed when the rules are ready. And to philosophize is this, to examine and confirm the rules; and then to use them when they are known is the act of a wise and good man.

EPICTETUS, *THE TEACHINGS OF A STOIC: SELECTED DISCOURSES AND THE ENCHIRIDION*, "WHAT THE BEGINNING OF PHILOSOPHY IS" (FROM C. EARLY 2ND CENTURY CE)

CHANGE

Observe constantly that all things take place by change, and accustom thyself to consider that the nature of the Universe loves nothing so much as to change the things which are and to make new things like them. For everything that exists is in a manner the seed of that which will be.

MARCUS AURELIUS, *MEDITATIONS*, "BOOK IV" (FROM C. 180 CE)

COOPERATION WITH NATURE

In every act observe the things which come first, and those which follow it; and so proceed to the act. If you do not, at first you will approach it with alacrity, without having thought of the things which will follow… My man, first of all consider what kind of thing it is; and then examine your own nature, if you are able to sustain the character. Do you wish to be a pentathlete or a wrestler? Look at your arms, your thighs, examine your loins. For different men are formed by nature for different things…

EPICTETUS, *THE TEACHINGS OF A STOIC: SELECTED DISCOURSES AND THE ENCHIRIDION*, "THE MANUAL: XXIX" (FROM C. EARLY 2ND CENTURY CE)

NOBILITY OF THOUGHT

"We must fix upon some good man and have him always before our eye as a witness of our life and actions." ... For sure, many sins would be prevented was some witness to be present at the commission. Let the mind, therefore, suppose someone present whom it may revere and from whole authority every secret may receive sanction. Happy the man who not only by his presence but by being thought upon has such influence upon another person as to induce him to act decently! And happy the man who so reverences another as upon only calling him to mind, forms and regulates his own conduct. He that so reverenceth another will soon be reverenced himself. Choose therefore Cato, or if Cato seems somewhat too rigid, choose Laelius, a man of not so severe a temper, or choose someone among your acquaintance whose life and manner of address charm you, and having in view either the understanding or presence of such a one, look upon him, either as your guardian or model. There must be someone, I say, according to whose plan we must form our morals. Without some certain rule you will never correct what is amiss.

LUCIUS SENECA, *LETTERS FROM A STOIC*, "XI. ON MODESTY, BASHFULNESS AND NATURAL HABIT" (FROM C. 63-65 CE)

DETACHMENT

Of things some are in our power, and others are not. In our power are opinion, movement towards a thing, desire, aversion, turning from a thing; and in a word, whatever are our acts. Not in our power are the body, property, reputation, offices (magisterial power), and in a word, whatever are not our own acts. And the things in our power are by nature free, not subject to restraint or hindrance; but the things not in our power are weak, slavish, subject to restraint, in the power of others. Remember then, that if you think the things which are by nature slavish to be free, and the things which are in the power of others to be your own, you will be hindered, you will lament, you will be disturbed, you will blame both gods and men; but if you think that only which is your own to be your own, and if you think that what is another's, as it really is, belongs to another, no man will ever compel you, no man will hinder you, you will never blame any man, you will accuse no man, you will do nothing involuntarily (against your will), no man will harm you, you will have no enemy, for you will not suffer any harm.

EPICTETUS, *THE TEACHINGS OF A STOIC: SELECTED DISCOURSES AND THE ENCHIRIDION*, "THE MANUAL: I"
(FROM C. EARLY 2ND CENTURY CE)

VIRTUE

No one ought to glory in what is not his own. We praise the vine whose branches are so loaded with fruit as to bend the very props to the ground with their burden. And would you prefer to this a vine with golden leaves and golden fruit? Fertility is the proper virtue of a vine. In man, likewise, that alone is commendable which is from himself. ... Commend that in him, which cannot be taken away from nor made a present to him. Do you ask what that is? The mind and reason perfected therein. For man is a rational animal, he has therefore completed his own proper good if accomplished according to the end for which he was born. And what is it that reason requires of him? The earliest thing in the world, only to live up to the dignity of his nature. But I own the common madness of the world makes this difficult. We push one another on to vice, and what hopes can there be of being restored to sanity while the people continue to drive us on and there is no friend to stop us in our career?

LUCIUS SENECA, *LETTERS FROM A STOIC*, "XLI. THERE IS A CERTAIN DIVINITY IN GOOD MEN" (FROM C. 63-65 CE)

GOODNESS

But my nature is rational and social; and my city and country, so far as I am Antoninus, is Rome, but so far as I am a man, it is the world. The things then which are useful to these cities are alone useful to me. Whatever happens to every man, this is for the interest of the universal: this might be sufficient. But further thou wilt observe this also as a general truth, if thou dost observe, that whatever is profitable to any man is profitable also to other men. But let the word profitable be taken here in the common sense as said of things of the middle kind, neither good nor bad.

MARCUS AURELIUS, *MEDITATIONS*, "BOOK VI" (FROM C. 180 CE)

DETACHMENT

…a disease may sometimes be prevented, or at least checked by timely medicine. For there is no disease but what hath its symptoms, particularly such as we have been subject to before. In short, any disease may be rendered tolerable by despising the last extremity that it threatens.

LUCIUS SENECA, *LETTERS FROM A STOIC*, "LXXVIII. ON SICKNESS, PAIN AND DEATH" (FROM C. 63-65 CE)

ACCEPTANCE

...he whom you love is mortal, and that what you love is nothing of your own; it has been given to you for the present, not that it should not be taken from you, nor has it been given to you for all time, but as a fig is given to you or a bunch of grapes at the appointed season of the year.

EPICTETUS, *THE TEACHINGS OF A STOIC: SELECTED DISCOURSES AND THE ENCHIRIDION*, "THE MANUAL: L" (FROM C. EARLY 2ND CENTURY CE)

TIME

What soul then has skill and knowledge? That which knows beginning and end, and knows the reason which pervades all substance and through all time by fixed periods [revolutions] administers the universe. Soon, very soon, thou wilt be ashes, or a skeleton, and either a name or not even a name; but name is sound and echo.

MARCUS AURELIUS, *MEDITATIONS*, "BOOK V" (FROM C. 180 CE)

NOBILITY OF THOUGHT

Whatever things (rules) are proposed to you (for the conduct of life) abide by them, as if they were laws, as if you would be guilty of impiety if you transgressed any of them. And whatever any man shall say about you, do not attend to it; for this is no affair of yours. How long will you then still defer thinking yourself worthy of the best things, and in no matter transgressing the distinctive reason? Have you accepted the theorems (rules), which it was your duty to agree to, and have you agreed to them? What teacher then do you still expect that you defer to him the correction of yourself? You are no longer a youth, but already a full-grown man.

EPICTETUS, *THE TEACHINGS OF A STOIC: SELECTED DISCOURSES AND THE ENCHIRIDION*, "THE MANUAL: L" (FROM C. EARLY 2ND CENTURY CE)

DETACHMENT

Thou wilt see all these things, people marrying, bringing up children, sick, dying, warring, feasting, trafficking, cultivating the ground, flattering, obstinately arrogant, suspecting, plotting, wishing for some to die, grumbling about the present, loving, heaping up treasure, desiring consulship, kingly power. Well then, that life of these people no longer exists at all. In like manner view also the other epochs of time and of whole nations, and see how many after great efforts soon fell and were resolved into the elements. But chiefly thou shouldst think of those whom thou hast thyself known distracting themselves about idle things, neglecting to do what was in accordance with their proper constitution, and to hold firmly to this and to be content with it. And herein it is necessary to remember that the attention given to everything has its proper value and proportion. For thus thou wilt not be dissatisfied, if thou appliest thyself to smaller matters no further than is fit.

MARCUS AURELIUS, *MEDITATIONS*, "BOOK IV" (FROM C. 180 CE)

WILL

You must be one man either good or bad; you must either labour at your own ruling faculty or at external things; you must either labour at things within or at external things; that is, you must either occupy the place of a philosopher or that of one of the vulgar.

EPICTETUS, *THE TEACHINGS OF A STOIC: SELECTED DISCOURSES AND THE ENCHIRIDION,* "THAT WE OUGHT TO PROCEED WITH CIRCUMSPECTION TO EVERYTHING" (FROM C. EARLY 2ND CENTURY CE)

NOBILITY OF THOUGHT

It is a dangerous habit also to approach obscene talk. When then, anything of this kind happens, if there is a good opportunity, rebuke the man who has proceeded to this talk; but if there is not an opportunity, by your silence at least, and blushing and expression of dissatisfaction by your countenance, show plainly that you are displeased at such talk.

EPICTETUS, *THE TEACHINGS OF A STOIC: SELECTED DISCOURSES AND THE ENCHIRIDION,* "THE MANUAL: XXXIII" (FROM C. EARLY 2ND CENTURY CE)

NOBILITY OF THOUGHT

"All things were lull'd by night, in pleasing rest," [says] the poet (Varro), but 'tis false, there can be no pleasing rest but what is the effect of reason. The night rather promotes than prevents trouble and only changes one scene of anxiety for another, for even the dreams of those that sleep are as turbulent as all the accidents of the day. There can be no true tranquillity but what ariseth from a sound mind. Behold the man who endeavours to sleep while the whole house is silent, and that the least noise may not reach his ears all the servants are ordered not to speak a word, and if they approach near his bed to tread as softly as possible, yet is he turning from one side to another and would fain get a nap, still complaining that he hears noises while not the least is made. Now what do you think is the reason of this? Why, his mind is disturbed, this must be appeased, the sedition within must be calmed, the noise is there for you must not think the mind is at peace, though the body were to lie as still as in the arms of death.

LUCIUS SENECA, *LETTERS FROM A STOIC*, "LVI. ON TRANQUILLITY" (FROM C. 63-65 CE)

TIME

For all things soon pass away and become a mere tale, and complete oblivion soon buries them. And I say this of those who have shone in a wondrous way. For the rest, as soon as they have breathed out their breath, they are gone, and no man speaks of them. And, to conclude the matter, what is even an eternal remembrance? A mere nothing. What then is that about which we ought to employ our serious pains? This one thing, thoughts just, and acts social, and words which never lie, and a disposition which gladly accepts all that happens, as necessary, as usual, as flowing from a principle and source of the same kind.

MARCUS AURELIUS, *MEDITATIONS*, "BOOK IV" (FROM C. 180 CE)

NOBILITY OF THOUGHT

Reflect upon such actions as were founded upon the principles of honour and virtue. Look upon yourself in the best light you can, call to memory such feats as you most admired in other men.

LUCIUS SENECA, *LETTERS FROM A STOIC*, "LXXVIII. ON SICKNESS, PAIN AND DEATH" (FROM C. 63-65 CE)

DETACHMENT

257

The disposition is light and wavering, which can be moved by any accidental found, it still retains anxiety and a dread of something that excites its curiosity and care… Know, therefore, you are then only truly composed when no alarm can move you, when no voice can shake you from yourself, whether it flatters or threatens you, or pours forth a variety of idle sounds.

LUCIUS SENECA, *LETTERS FROM A STOIC*, "LVI. ON TRANQUILLITY" (FROM C. 63-65 CE)

WILL

258

I was quite emaciated and began to think that life was not worth preserving, but the old age of a most indulgent father checked the daring thought, for I considered not so much how resolutely I could die myself, but that the loss of me would necessarily afflict my father. I was therefore determined to struggle for life. For even this is *sometimes* a manly design.

LUCIUS SENECA, *LETTERS FROM A STOIC*, "LXXVIII. ON SICKNESS, PAIN AND DEATH" (FROM C. 63-65 CE)

GOODNESS

There is only one way to happiness, and let this rule be ready both in the morning and during the day and by night: the rule is not to look towards things which are out of the power of our will, to think that nothing is our own, to give up all things to the Divinity, to Fortune... for a man to observe that only which is his own, that which cannot be hindered; and when we read, to refer our reading to this only, and our writing and our listening. For never commend a man on account of these things which are common to all, but on account of his opinions (principles); for these are the things which belong to each man, which make his actions bad or good.

EPICTETUS, *THE TEACHINGS OF A STOIC: SELECTED DISCOURSES AND THE ENCHIRIDION*, "TO THOSE WHO ARE DESIROUS OF PASSING LIFE IN TRANQUILITY" (FROM C. EARLY 2ND CENTURY CE)

WISDOM

If you were ill, you would not concern yourself with family affairs, nor with the business of the Forum, nor would you have so great a value for anyone as to appear an advocate in court for him. Your whole attention would be taken up in endeavouring to get rid of your disorder, and will you not do the same now? Let every impediment be thrown aside while you attend only to the attainment of a sound mind. No one can attain this who is busied about other things. Philosophy exerciseth a regal power, she grants time but accepts it not. She is no substitute, she is the principal in waiting and gives commands.

LUCIUS SENECA, *LETTERS FROM A STOIC*, "LIII. ON THE GREAT POWER AND VALUE OF PHILOSOPHY" (FROM C. 63-65 CE)

COOPERATION WITH NATURE

Well then God constitutes every animal, one to be eaten, another to serve for agriculture, another to supply cheese, and another for some like use; for which purposes what need is there to understand appearances and to be able to distinguish them? But God has introduced man to be a spectator of God and of his works; and not only a spectator of them, but an interpreter. For this reason it is shameful for man to begin and to end where irrational animals do; but rather he ought to begin where they begin, and to end where nature ends in us; and nature ends in contemplation and understanding, and in a way of life conformable to nature. Take care then not to die without having been spectators of these things.

EPICTETUS, *THE TEACHINGS OF A STOIC: SELECTED DISCOURSES AND THE ENCHIRIDION*, "OF PROVIDENCE" (FROM C. EARLY 2ND CENTURY CE)

DETACHMENT

Occupy thyself with few things, says the philosopher, if thou wouldst be tranquil – But consider if it would not be better to say, Do what is necessary, and whatever the reason of the animal which is naturally social requires, and as it requires. For this brings not only the tranquility which comes from doing well, but also that which comes from doing few things. For the greatest part of what we say and do being unnecessary, if a man takes this away, he will have more leisure and less uneasiness. Accordingly on every occasion a man should ask himself, Is this one of the unnecessary things? Now a man should take away not only unnecessary acts, but also, unnecessary thoughts, for thus superfluous acts will not follow after.

MARCUS AURELIUS, *MEDITATIONS*, "BOOK IV" (FROM C. 180 CE)

NOBILITY OF THOUGHT

If a thing is difficult to be accomplished by thyself, do not think that it is impossible for man: but if anything is possible for man and conformable to his nature, think that this can be attained by thyself too.

MARCUS AURELIUS, *MEDITATIONS*, "BOOK VI" (FROM C. 180 CE)

DETACHMENT

Then after receiving everything from another and even yourself, are you angry and do you blame the giver if he takes anything from you? Who are you, and for what purpose did you come into the world? Did not he (God) introduce you here, did he not show you the light, did he not give you fellow-workers, and perceptions and reason? And as whom did he introduce you here? Did he not introduce you as subject to death, and as one to live on the Earth with a little flesh, and to observe his administration, and to join with him in the spectacle and the festival for a short time? Will you not then, as long as you have been permitted, after seeing the spectacle and the solemnity, when he leads you out, go with adoration of him and thanks for what you have heard and seen? … For what purpose then have I received these things? To use them. How long? So long as he who has lent them chooses. What if they are necessary to me? Do not attach yourself to them and they will not be necessary; do not say to yourself that they are necessary, and then they are not necessary.

EPICTETUS, *THE TEACHINGS OF A STOIC: SELECTED DISCOURSES AND THE ENCHIRIDION*, "TO THOSE WHO FALL OFF (DESIST) FROM THEIR PURPOSE" (FROM C. EARLY 2ND CENTURY CE)

NOBILITY OF THOUGHT

But why, you say, do I delight to spend my time in these futile enquiries, which check not any fond desire nor drive from the bosom an irregular passion? Truly, I employ myself on these subjects in order to settle my mind and fix my attention. I first pry into and examine myself, then turn my thoughts to the vast world. Nor in this employ do I lose my time as you imagine, for all these things if they are not minced too minutely and spun out in vain and useless subtleties mightily raise and refresh the soul, which being heavily pressed down by its usual burden desires to be at large and to return thither from whence it was taken. For this body is the load and punishment of the soul. The soul perpetually labours under the weight of it, it is actually in bonds until philosophy comes to its relief, permits it to breathe a while and delight itself with the vast prospect of nature, and to transfer the affections from things below to things above, from the terrestrial to such as are heavenly.

LUCIUS SENECA, *LETTERS FROM A STOIC*, "LXV. ON THE FIRST CAUSE" (FROM C. 63-65 CE)

DETACHMENT

I consist of a little body and a soul. Now to this little body all things are indifferent, for it is not able to perceive differences. But to the understanding those things only are indifferent, which are not the works of its own activity. But whatever things are the works of its own activity, all these are in its power. And of these however only those which are done with reference to the present; for as to the future and the past activities of the mind, even these are for the present indifferent.

MARCUS AURELIUS, *MEDITATIONS*, "BOOK VI" (FROM C. 180 CE)

CHANGE

We see that the carpenter when he has learned certain things becomes a carpenter; the pilot by learning certain things becomes a pilot. May it not then in philosophy also not be sufficient to wish to be wise and good, and that there is also a necessity to learn certain things? We inquire then what these things are.

EPICTETUS, *THE TEACHINGS OF A STOIC: SELECTED DISCOURSES AND THE ENCHIRIDION*, "TO NASO" (FROM C. EARLY 2ND CENTURY CE)

ACCEPTANCE

Nothing is distasteful when we have got over the fear of death. There are three things which in every disease are grievous. The fear of death, the pain of the body and the intermission of pleasures. Of death we have said enough already, I shall only add that this fear proceeds not from the disease but from nature itself. A disease hath often prevented death, and the very thoughts of dying have contributed to health. You will die not because you are sick but because you live. Be you ever so well recovered, death still expects you. You have not escaped death but only such a fit of sickness.

LUCIUS SENECA, *LETTERS FROM A STOIC*, "LXXVIII. ON SICKNESS, PAIN AND DEATH" (FROM C. 63-65 CE)

COOPERATION WITH NATURE

All things are implicated with one another, and the bond is holy; there is hardly anything unconnected with any other thing. For things have been coordinated, and they combine to form the same universe [order].

MARCUS AURELIUS, *MEDITATIONS*, "BOOK VII" (FROM C. 180 CE)

COOPERATION WITH NATURE

What then is the punishment of those who do not accept? It is to be what they are. Is any person dissatisfied with being alone? Let him be alone. Is a man dissatisfied with his parents? Let him be a bad son, and lament. Is he dissatisfied with his children? Let him be a bad father. Cast him into prison. What prison? Where he is already, for he is there against his will; and where a man is against his will, there he is in prison. So Socrates was not in prison, for he was there willingly. Must my leg then be lamed? Wretch, do you then on account of one poor leg find fault with the world? Will you not willingly surrender it for the whole? Will you not withdraw from it? Will you not gladly part with it to him who gave it?

EPICTETUS, *THE TEACHINGS OF A STOIC: SELECTED DISCOURSES AND THE ENCHIRIDION,* "OF PROVIDENCE" (FROM C. EARLY 2ND CENTURY CE)

WISDOM

What is the first business of him who philosophizes? To throw away self-conceit. For it is impossible for a man to begin to learn that which he thinks that he knows. As to things then which ought to be done and ought not to be done, and good and bad, and beautiful and ugly, all of us talking of them at random go to the philosophers; and on these matters we praise, we censure, we accuse, we blame, we judge and determine about principles honorable and dishonorable. But why do we go to the philosophers? Because we wish to learn what we do not think that we know.

EPICTETUS, *THE TEACHINGS OF A STOIC: SELECTED DISCOURSES AND THE ENCHIRIDION*, "THAT WE DO NOT STRIVE TO USE OUR OPINIONS ABOUT GOOD AND EVIL" (FROM C. EARLY 2ND CENTURY CE)

DETACHMENT

Think not so much of what thou hast not as of what thou hast: but of the things which thou hast select the best, and then reflect how eagerly they would have been sought, if thou hadst them not.

MARCUS AURELIUS, *MEDITATIONS*, "BOOK VII" (FROM C. 180 CE)

NOBILITY OF THOUGHT

Weak and frail, we subsist as it were by intervals; let us set our minds then upon the things that are eternal, let us admire the universal forms of things, flying on high, and God in the midst of them, disposing all things as it seemeth best and providing (as he could not make them immortal, because formed of matter) that they perish not in death but through his wisdom overcome the malignity of body. For all things remain not because they are eternal, but because they are under the care and protection of an Almighty governor. Things immortal in their own nature stand not in need of a guardian, but mortal things are preserved by the hand that made them, surmounting the frailty of the materials by his almighty power.

LUCIUS SENECA, *LETTERS FROM A STOIC*, "LVIII. ON THE POVERTY OF THE LATIN TONGUE" (FROM C. 63-65 CE)

ACCEPTANCE

If a man possesses any superiority, or thinks that he does when he does not, such a man, if he is uninstructed, will of necessity be puffed up through it. For instance, the tyrant says, I am master of all! And what can you do for me? Can you give me desire which shall have no hindrance? How can you? Have you the infallible power of avoiding what you would avoid? Have you the power of moving towards an object without error? And how do you possess this power? Come, when you are in a ship, do you trust to yourself or to the helmsman? And when you are in a chariot, to whom do you trust but to the driver? And how is it in all other arts? Just the same.

EPICTETUS, *THE TEACHINGS OF A STOIC: SELECTED DISCOURSES AND THE ENCHIRIDION*, "HOW WE SHOULD BEHAVE TO TYRANTS" (FROM C. EARLY 2ND CENTURY CE)

DETACHMENT

Keep by every means what is your own; do not desire what belongs to others. Fidelity (integrity) is your own, virtuous shame is your own; who then can take these things from you? Who else than yourself will hinder you from using them? But how do you act? When you seek what is not your own, you lose that which is your own.

EPICTETUS, *THE TEACHINGS OF A STOIC: SELECTED DISCOURSES AND THE ENCHIRIDION*, "HOW WE SHOULD STRUGGLE WITH CIRCUMSTANCES" (FROM C. EARLY 2ND CENTURY CE)

COOPERATION WITH NATURE

One man after burying another has been laid out dead, and another buries him: and all this in a short time. To conclude, always observe how ephemeral and worthless human things are, and what was yesterday a little mucus tomorrow will be a mummy or ashes. Pass then through this little space of time conformably to nature, and end thy journey in content, just as an olive falls off when it is ripe, blessing nature who produced it, and thanking the tree on which it grew.

MARCUS AURELIUS, *MEDITATIONS*, "BOOK IV" (FROM C. 180 CE)

DETACHMENT

Why then are we angry? Is it because we value so much the things of which these men rob us? Do not admire your clothes, and then you will not be angry with the thief. Consider this matter thus: you have fine clothes; your neighbour has not; you have a window; you wish to air the clothes. The thief does not know wherein man's good consists, but he thinks that it consists in having fine clothes, the very thing which you also think. Must he not then come and take them away? When you show a cake to greedy persons, and swallow it all yourself, do you expect them not to snatch it from you? Do not provoke them…

EPICTETUS, *THE TEACHINGS OF A STOIC: SELECTED DISCOURSES AND THE ENCHIRIDION*, "THAT WE OUGHT NOT TO BE ANGRY WITH THE ERRORS (FAULTS) OF OTHERS" (FROM C. EARLY 2ND CENTURY CE)

TIME

Let not future things disturb thee, for thou wilt come to them, if it shall be necessary, having with thee the same reason which now thou usest for present things.

MARCUS AURELIUS, *MEDITATIONS*, "BOOK VII" (FROM C. 180 CE)

CHANGE

Man, consider first what the matter is (which you propose to do), then your own nature also, what it is able to bear. If you are a wrestler, look at your shoulders, your thighs, your loins: for different men are naturally formed for different things. Do you think that, if you do (what you are doing daily), you can be a philosopher? Do you think that you can eat as you do now, drink as you do now, and in the same way be angry and out of humour? You must watch, labour, conquer certain desires... When you have considered all these things completely, then, if you think proper, approach to philosophy, if you would gain in exchange for these things freedom from perturbations, liberty, tranquillity.

EPICTETUS, *THE TEACHINGS OF A STOIC: SELECTED DISCOURSES AND THE ENCHIRIDION*, "THAT WE OUGHT TO PROCEED WITH CIRCUMSPECTION TO EVERYTHING" (FROM C. EARLY 2ND CENTURY CE)

VIRTUE

Hence it is manifest that a mind that is tender and not over tenacious of what is right is not to be entrusted with the converse of the many. Vice is catching. The varying populace can shake Socrates, a Cato or a Laelius from his purpose, so that none of us, however polished the disposition, can stand against the violence of vices that assail us in such a numerous body. Nay, even one example of luxury or avarice is capable of doing much mischief. A delicate coxcomb by degrees softens… his conversants, a rich neighbour incites covetousness, an ill-minded man is apt to taint with malignity his companion, however simple and candid. What then, think you, must be the consequence when a man subjects himself to every public attack? You must either imitate or hate the assailants. Both are to be avoided; if left you become like the bad, because they are many, or inimical to many because unlike them.

LUCIUS SENECA, *LETTERS FROM A STOIC*, "VII. ON PUBLIC SHOWS, PARTICULARLY THE GLADIATORS – AND CONVERSE WITH THE WORLD" (FROM C. 63-65 CE)

DETACHMENT

Be not elated at any advantage (excellence) which belongs to another. If a horse when he is elated should say, I am beautiful, one might endure it. But when you are elated, and say, I have a beautiful horse, you must know that you are elated at having a good horse. What then is your own? The use of appearances. Consequently when in the use of appearances you are conformable to nature, then be elated, for then you will be elated at something good which is your own.

EPICTETUS, *THE TEACHINGS OF A STOIC: SELECTED DISCOURSES AND THE ENCHIRIDION*, "THE MANUAL: VI" (FROM C. EARLY 2ND CENTURY CE)

COOPERATION WITH NATURE

Constantly regard the universe as one living being, having one substance and one soul; and observe how all things have reference to one perception, the perception of this one living being; and how all things act with one movement; and how all things are the cooperating causes of all things which exist; observe too the continuous spinning of the thread and the contexture of the web.

MARCUS AURELIUS, *MEDITATIONS*, "BOOK IV" (FROM C. 180 CE)

VIRTUE

The wise man, I was saying, however satisfied in himself is yet desirous to have a friend, and for this reason was there no other that so great a virtue as the exercise of friendship may not lie dormant. Not, as Epicurus says in the Epistle before me, that he may have a friend to comfort him on the bed of sickness or relieve him when poor or in prison, but that he may have someone on whom to display the like merciful disposition, whether by comforting him in sickness or delivering him from inimical durance. He thinks very wrong who regards only himself and makes self-interest the ground of friendship, he will end as he began. He professes to serve his friend even in bonds, but as soon as he hears the clinking of the chain, deserts him.

LUCIUS SENECA, *LETTERS FROM A STOIC*, "IX. ON FRIENDSHIP, SELF-COMPLACENCY AND CONTENTMENT" (FROM C. 63-65 CE)

VIRTUE

This is the chief thing: Be not perturbed, for all things are according to the nature of the universal; and in a little time thou wilt be nobody and nowhere, like Hadrian and Augustus. In the next place having fixed thy eyes steadily on thy business look at it, and at the same time remembering that it is thy duty to be a good man, and what man's nature demands, do that without turning aside; and speak as it seems to thee most just, only let it be with a good disposition and with modesty and without hypocrisy.

MARCUS AURELIUS, *MEDITATIONS*, "BOOK VIII" (FROM C. 180 CE)

WILL

Set apart certain days in which taking up with the meanest and vilest diet and the most coarse and rough clothing you may say to yourself, "and is this all that I was afraid of?" While in security let the mind prepare itself against difficulties, and amidst the favours of fortune be strengthened against any injurious treatment. The soldier in the time of peace exercises himself, throws up trenches and in fruitless labour takes a great deal of pains to inure himself against the time when it may become necessary. Whom you would not have tremble in the time of action you must harden before the time comes.

LUCIUS SENECA, *LETTERS FROM A STOIC*, "XVIII. ON THE BEHAVIOUR OF A PHILOSOPHER AT CERTAIN SEASONS. ON POVERTY AND IMMODERATE ANGER" (FROM C. 63-65 CE)

NOBILITY OF THOUGHT

Send us your thoughts, a man may very well converse with his absent friends, indeed as often and as long as you please. Nay, we enjoy this pleasure, great as it is, the more on the account of absence, for the being present is apt to make us somewhat shy, and because having an opportunity to talk and walk together when we sit down, or are parted, we think no more of those we saw so lately, and what may make us bear absence the more patiently is there is no one who is not often absent to his friend or neighbour. For consider the many absent nights and the different employs of the day on either side and the different pursuits, the different studies and frequent calls out of the city and you will find that a voyage or a journey does not deprive us of much of our friend's company as you imagined.

LUCIUS SENECA, *LETTERS FROM A STOIC*, "LV. A TRUE FRIEND IS NEVER ABSENT" (FROM C. 63-65 CE)

DETACHMENT

…how ridiculous is it to fear anything, more or less, when there is one common end of all? For what matter is it whether a man be killed by the falling of a tower or of a mountain? It is still but death, nothing more, yet there are some who are more afraid of one thing than another, though they are both alike fatal. Fear is therefore more apprehensive of the cause than of the effect.

LUCIUS SENECA, *LETTERS FROM A STOIC*, "LVII. ON FEAR AND THE IMMORTALITY OF THE SOUL" (FROM C. 63-65 CE)

ACCEPTANCE

Let it make no difference to thee whether thou art cold or warm, if thou art doing thy duty; and whether thou art drowsy or satisfied with sleep; and whether ill-spoken of or praised; and whether dying or doing something else. For it is one of the acts of life, this act by which we die: it is sufficient then in this act also to do well what we have in hand.

MARCUS AURELIUS, *MEDITATIONS*, "BOOK VI" (FROM C. 180 CE)

NOBILITY OF THOUGHT

…they utter these useless words from their real opinions; but you utter your elegant words only from your lips; for this reason they are without strength and dead, and it is nauseous to listen to your exhortations and your miserable virtue, which is talked of everywhere (up and down). In this way the vulgar have the advantage over you; for every opinion is strong and invincible. Until then the good sentiments are fixed in you, and you shall have acquired a certain power for your security, I advise you to be careful in your association with common persons; if you are not, every day like wax in the sun there will be melted away whatever you inscribe on your minds in the school.

EPICTETUS, *THE TEACHINGS OF A STOIC: SELECTED DISCOURSES AND THE ENCHIRIDION*, "THAT WE OUGHT WITH CAUTION TO ENTER INTO FAMILIAR INTERCOURSE WITH MEN" (FROM C. EARLY 2ND CENTURY CE)

COOPERATION WITH NATURE

The universe is either a confusion, and a mutual involution of things, and a dispersion; or it is unity and order and providence. If then it is the former, why do I desire to tarry in a fortuitous combination of things and such a disorder? And why do I care about anything else than how I shall at last become earth? And why am I disturbed, for the dispersion of my elements will happen whatever I do. But if the other supposition is true, I venerate, and I am firm, and I trust in him who governs.

MARCUS AURELIUS, *MEDITATIONS*, "BOOK VI" (FROM C. 180 CE)

GOODNESS

When thou hast done a good act and another has received it, why dost thou look for a third thing besides these, as fools do, either to have the reputation of having done a good act or to obtain a return? No man is tired of receiving what is useful. But it is useful to act according to nature. Do not then be tired of receiving what is useful by doing it to others.

MARCUS AURELIUS, *MEDITATIONS*, "BOOK VII"
(FROM C. 180 CE)

WILL

...this is the law of nature and of God that the superior shall always overpower the inferior. In what? In that in which it is superior. One body is stronger than another: many are stronger than one: the thief is stronger than he who is not a thief... a man has seized me by the cloak, and is drawing me to the public place: then others bawl out, Philosopher, what has been the use of your opinions? See, you are dragged to prison, you are going to be beheaded. And what system of philosophy could I have made so that, if a stronger man should have laid hold of my cloak, I should not be dragged off; that if ten men should have laid hold of me and cast me into prison, I should not be cast in? Have I learned nothing else then? I have learned to see that everything which happens, if it be independent of my will, is nothing to me.

EPICTETUS, *THE TEACHINGS OF A STOIC: SELECTED DISCOURSES AND THE ENCHIRIDION*, "ON CONSTANCY (OR FIRMNESS)" (FROM C. EARLY 2ND CENTURY CE)

VIRTUE

These are what are commonly called temporary friendships, which last no longer than to serve a turn. Hence the prosperous are surrounded with a number of friends, while the wretched bemoan themselves in solitude. For then is the time of flight, when put to the trial. From whence we see so many scandalous examples of friends, either deserting or betraying one another through fear…

LUCIUS SENECA, *LETTERS FROM A STOIC*, "IX. ON FRIENDSHIP, SELF-COMPLACENCY AND CONTENTMENT" (FROM C. 63-65 CE)

GOODNESS

For now who among us is not able to discourse according to the rules of art about good and evil things (in this fashion)? That of things some are good, and some are bad, and some are indifferent: the good then are virtues, and the things which participate in virtues; and the bad are the contrary; and the indifferent are wealth, health, reputation.

EPICTETUS, *THE TEACHINGS OF A STOIC: SELECTED DISCOURSES AND THE ENCHIRIDION*, "THAT WHEN WE CANNOT FULFIL THAT WHICH THE CHARACTER OF A MAN PROMISES, WE ASSUME THE CHARACTER OF A PHILOSOPHER" (FROM C. EARLY 2ND CENTURY CE)

WISDOM

The hypothetical proposition is indifferent: the judgment about it is not indifferent, but it is either knowledge or opinion or error. Thus life is indifferent: the use is not indifferent. When any man then tells you that these things also are indifferent, do not become negligent; and when a man invites you to be careful (about such things), do not become abject and struck with admiration of material things. And it is good for you to know your own preparation and power, that in those matters where you have not been prepared, you may keep quiet, and not be vexed, if others have the advantage over you. For you too in syllogisms will claim to have the advantage over them; and if others should be vexed at this, you will console them by saying, "I have learned them, and you have not." Thus also where there is need of any practice, seek not that which is acquired from the need (of such practice), but yield in that matter to those who have had practice, and be yourself content with firmness of mind.

EPICTETUS, *THE TEACHINGS OF A STOIC: SELECTED DISCOURSES AND THE ENCHIRIDION*, "OF INDIFFERENCE" (FROM C. EARLY 2ND CENTURY CE)

DETACHMENT

…where there are things which appear most worthy of our approbation, we ought to lay them bare and look at their worthlessness and strip them of all the words by which they are exalted. For outward show is a wonderful perverter of the reason, and when thou art most sure that thou art employed about things worth thy pains, it is then that it cheats thee most.

MARCUS AURELIUS, *MEDITATIONS*, "BOOK VI" (FROM C. 180 CE)

NOBILITY OF THOUGHT

Will you not then seek the nature of good in the rational animal? For if it is not there, you will not choose to say that it exists in any other thing (plant or animal). What then? Are not plants and animals also the works of God? They are; but they are not superior things, nor yet parts of the gods. But you are a superior thing; you are a portion separated from the Deity; you have in yourself a certain portion of him. Why then are you ignorant of your own noble descent?

EPICTETUS, *THE TEACHINGS OF A STOIC: SELECTED DISCOURSES AND THE ENCHIRIDION*, "HOW WE OUGHT TO USE DIVINATION" (FROM C. EARLY 2ND CENTURY CE)

DETACHMENT

Confidence (courage) then ought to be employed against death, and caution against the fear of death. But now we do the contrary, and employ against death the attempt to escape; and to our opinion about it we employ carelessness, rashness, and indifference. These things Socrates properly used to call tragic masks; for as to children masks appear terrible and fearful from inexperience, we also are affected in like manner by events (the things which happen in life) for no other reason than children are by masks. For what is a child? Ignorance. What is a child? Want of knowledge. For when a child knows these things, he is in no way inferior to us. What is death? A tragic mask. Turn it and examine it. See, it does not bite. The poor body must be separated from the spirit either now or later as it was separated from it before. Why then are you troubled if it be separated now? For if it is not separated now, it will be separated afterwards…

EPICTETUS, *THE TEACHINGS OF A STOIC: SELECTED DISCOURSES AND THE ENCHIRIDION*, "THAT CONFIDENCE (COURAGE) IS NOT INCONSISTENT WITH CAUTION" (FROM C. EARLY 2ND CENTURY CE)

VIRTUE

Freedom. For in these matters we must not believe the many, who say that free persons only ought to be educated, but we should rather believe the philosophers who say that the educated only are free. How is this? In this manner: Is freedom anything else than the power of living as we choose? Nothing else. Tell me then, ye men, do you wish to live in error? We do not. No one then who lives in error is free. Do you wish to live in fear? Do you wish to live in sorrow? Do you wish to live in perturbation? By no means. No one then who is in a state of fear or sorrow or perturbation is free; but whoever is delivered from sorrows and fears and perturbations, he is at the same time also delivered from servitude… For philosophers say we allow none to be free except the educated; that is, God does not allow it.

EPICTETUS, *THE TEACHINGS OF A STOIC: SELECTED DISCOURSES AND THE ENCHIRIDION*, "THAT CONFIDENCE (COURAGE) IS NOT INCONSISTENT WITH CAUTION" (FROM C. EARLY 2ND CENTURY CE)

COOPERATION WITH NATURE

Every instrument, tool, vessel, if it does that for which it has been made, is well, and yet he who made it is not there. But in the things which are held together by nature there is within and there abides in them the power which made them; wherefore the more is it fit to reverence this power, and to think, that, if thou dost live and act according to its will, everything in thee is in conformity to intelligence. And thus also in the universe the things which belong to it are in conformity to intelligence.

MARCUS AURELIUS, *MEDITATIONS*, "BOOK VI" (FROM C. 180 CE)

DETACHMENT

Then examine it (things) by the rules which you possess, and by this first and chiefly, whether it relates to the things which are in our power or to things which are not in our power; and if it relates to anything which is not in our power, be ready to say that it does not concern you.

EPICTETUS, *THE TEACHINGS OF A STOIC: SELECTED DISCOURSES AND THE ENCHIRIDION*, "THE MANUAL: I" (FROM C. EARLY 2ND CENTURY CE)

COOPERATION WITH NATURE

But to return to what is properly disagreeable and irksome in this respect. A disease is generally attended with great pains, yet some intervals make even these tolerable. And the more intense the pain is, the sooner it comes to an end. No one can suffer any torture long. Kind nature hath been so indulgent to us as to make our pains either tolerable or short.

LUCIUS SENECA, *LETTERS FROM A STOIC*, "LXXVIII. ON SICKNESS, PAIN AND DEATH" (FROM C. 63-65 CE)

DETACHMENT

Remember that not only the desire of power and of riches makes us mean and subject to others, but even the desire of tranquillity, and of leisure, and of travelling abroad, and of learning. For, to speak plainly, whatever the external thing may be, the value which we set upon it places us in subjection to others.

EPICTETUS, *THE TEACHINGS OF A STOIC: SELECTED DISCOURSES AND THE ENCHIRIDION*, "TO THOSE WHO FALL OFF (DESIST) FROM THEIR PURPOSE" (FROM C. EARLY 2ND CENTURY CE)

VIRTUE

For my own part, as if I was now about to make the experiment and the day approached that must pass sentence on the foregoing years, I thus observe and commune with myself. "All that I have said or done hitherto is nothing. Vain and deceitful are the assurances of the mind, all involved in chicane and flattery. What advance I made in wisdom death alone can show. I therefore calmly compose myself against that day when all shifts and subtleties laid aside I must pronounce truly concerning myself, whether I speak and think what is truly great and noble. Whether the big and contemptuous words thrown out against fortune were mere dissimulation and artifice to engage applause. Regard not the opinion of men, 'tis at best doubtful and generally partial. Regard not particular studies, our business relates to the whole of life, death will pronounce sentence on the man…"

LUCIUS SENECA, *LETTERS FROM A STOIC*, "XXVII. ON GOOD OLD AGE. MEDITATION ON DEATH" (FROM C. 63-65 CE)

COOPERATION WITH NATURE

What are you? A man. If you consider yourself as detached from other men, it is according to nature to live to old age, to be rich, to be healthy. But if you consider yourself as a man and a part of a certain whole, it is for the sake of that whole that at one time you should be sick, at another time take a voyage and run into danger, and at another time be in want, and in some cases die prematurely. Why then are you troubled? Do you not know, that as a foot is no longer a foot if it is detached from the body, so you are no longer a man if you are separated from other men. For what is a man? A part of a state, of that first which consists of gods and of men; then of that which is called next to it, which is a small image of the universal state.

EPICTETUS, *THE TEACHINGS OF A STOIC: SELECTED DISCOURSES AND THE ENCHIRIDION*, "OF TRANQUILITY (FREEDOM FROM PERTURBATION)"
(FROM C. EARLY 2ND CENTURY CE)

CHANGE

If souls continue to exist, how does the air contain them from eternity? But how does the earth contain the bodies of those who have been buried from time so remote? For as here the mutation of these bodies after a certain continuance, whatever it may be, and their dissolution make room for other dead bodies; so the souls which are removed into the air after subsisting for some time are transmuted and diffused, and assume a fiery nature by being received into the seminal intelligence of the universe, and in this way make room for the fresh souls which come to dwell there. And this is the answer which a man might give on the hypothesis of souls continuing to exist.

MARCUS AURELIUS, *MEDITATIONS*, "BOOK IV" (FROM C. 180 CE)

WISDOM

Wipe out the imagination. Stop the pulling of the strings. Confine thyself to the present. Understand well what happens either to thee or to another.

MARCUS AURELIUS, *MEDITATIONS*, "BOOK VII" (FROM C. 180 CE)

WISDOM

But someone will say, "what avails philosophy, if fate (or destiny as the Stoics think) will take its course, if God is the supreme governor of the world? Or if (according to the Epicureans) Chance is all in all, for things certain cannot be altered, and no preparation can be made against what is uncertain if either God hath prevented my purposes and hath decreed what I shall do, or if every event is in the disposal of Fortune?" Be this as it will, Lucilius, let any or all of these opinions take place, philosophy is nevertheless necessary and to be diligently studied. Whether Fate, I say, binds us by an inexorable law, or God, the sovereign of the world, disposeth all things, or Chance impels and tosseth about at random human affairs, still philosophy must be our defence. This will exhort us to obey God with a willing mind and more strenuously to resist the power of Fortune. This will teach you to trust in providence and humbly submit to casualties.

LUCIUS SENECA, *LETTERS FROM A STOIC*, "XVI. ON THE STUDY OF PHILOSOPHY" (FROM C. 63-65 CE)

DETACHMENT

In like manner some have continually so inured themselves to poverty as almost to proceed to want, that they may never be surprised with what they have learned to bear… Yet after all, there is no reason to think you have done a great thing. It is no more than what many thousand slaves and poor wretches do daily. All that you can boast of is that you do it voluntarily. And then it will be as easy for you to endure it always as sometimes to undergo the trial. Let us be exercised, as it were, at the post, lest fortune should come upon us unprepared. Let poverty be familiar to us. We shall more securely enjoy wealth if we know that it is not grievous to be poor.

LUCIUS SENECA, *LETTERS FROM A STOIC*, "XVIII. ON THE BEHAVIOUR OF A PHILOSOPHER AT CERTAIN SEASONS. ON POVERTY AND IMMODERATE ANGER" (FROM C. 63-65 CE)

WISDOM

The wise man, and even the disciple of wisdom, remains indeed still in the body, yet the better part of him frequently makes excursions. All his thoughts are set upon sublime things, and as if bound by the military oath he looks on the gift of life as his present pay and so reforms himself as to have neither love nor hatred thereto, and from hence patiently endures all that mortality is subject to, well knowing that greater and more solid satisfactions are yet to come.

LUCIUS SENECA, *LETTERS FROM A STOIC*, "LXV. ON THE FIRST CAUSE" (FROM C. 63-65 CE)

VIRTUE

In the mind of one who is chastened and purified thou wilt find no corrupt matter, nor impurity, nor any sore skinned over. Nor is his life incomplete when fate overtakes him, as one may say of an actor who leaves the stage before ending and finishing the play. Besides, there is in him nothing servile, nor affected, nor too closely bound to other things, nor yet detached from other things, nothing worthy of blame, nothing which seeks a hiding-place.

MARCUS AURELIUS, *MEDITATIONS*, "BOOK III" (FROM C. 180 CE)

COOPERATION WITH NATURE

So long as future things are uncertain, I always cling to those which are more adapted to the conservation of that which is according to nature; for God himself has given me the faculty of such choice. But if I knew that it was fated (in the order of things) for me to be sick, I would even move towards it... For why are ears of corn produced? Is it not that they may become dry? And do they not become dry that they may be reaped? For they are not separated from communion with other things. If then they had perception, ought they to wish never to be reaped? But this is a curse upon ears of corn to be never reaped. So we must know that in the case of men too it is a curse not to die, just the same as not to be ripened and not to be reaped. But since we must be reaped, and we also know that we are reaped, we are vexed at it; for we neither know what we are nor have we studied what belongs to man...

EPICTETUS, *THE TEACHINGS OF A STOIC: SELECTED DISCOURSES AND THE ENCHIRIDION*, "OF INDIFFERENCE" (FROM C. EARLY 2ND CENTURY CE)

CHANGE

Some things are hurrying into existence, and others are hurrying out of it; and of that which is coming into existence part is already extinguished. Motions and changes are continually renewing the world, just as the uninterrupted course of time is always renewing the infinite duration of ages. In this flowing stream then, on which there is no abiding, what is there of the things which hurry by on which a man would set a high price? It would be just as if a man should fall in love with one of the sparrows which fly by, but it has already passed out of sight. Something of this kind is the very life of every man, like the exhalation of the blood and the respiration of the air. For such as it is to have once drawn in the air and to have given it back, which we do every moment, just the same is it with the whole respiratory power, which thou didst receive at thy birth yesterday and the day before, to give it back to the element from which thou didst first draw it.

MARCUS AURELIUS, *MEDITATIONS*, "BOOK VI" (FROM C. 180 CE)

NOBILITY OF THOUGHT

And would you, Lucilius, debar me from an inspection into the works of nature and confine me from a view of the whole to some scanty part of it? Shall I not enquire into the origin of things, who created the universe, who first divided the mass and gave motion to inert and lifeless matter? Shall I not enquire who formed this our world, by what wisdom such an immensity of things came under rule and order, who collected the scattered and separated such as were confused and blended together, and brought forth the wonderful beauty that lay concealed under one squalid deformity or chaos? ... Shall I not enquire, I say, after these things? Shall I remain forever ignorant whence I came, and whether I am to see this world but once or often? Whether I am going and what happy mansion waits the soul when delivered from the servitude of the body? Do you forbid me to concern myself with heaven, i.e., do you command me to live with my head ever bowed down to the earth? No, I am greater and born to nobler purposes than to be the vile bondslave of my body, which I consider in no other light than as the chain that deprives me of my native liberty. This body then let Fortune attack when she pleases, she cannot wound me through it. All that can suffer in me is the body. Subject as this tabernacle is to injury, the soul that dwells therein is still free.

LUCIUS SENECA, *LETTERS FROM A STOIC*, "LXV. ON THE FIRST CAUSE" (FROM C. 63-65 CE)

VIRTUE

Such will I show myself to you, faithful, modest, noble, free from perturbation. What, and immortal, too, except from old age, and from sickness? No, but dying as becomes a god, sickening as becomes a god. This power I possess; this I can do. But the rest I do not possess, nor can I do. I will show the nerves (strength) of a philosopher. What nerves are these? A desire never disappointed, an aversion which never falls on that which it would avoid, a proper pursuit, a diligent purpose, an assent which is not rash. These you shall see.

EPICTETUS, *THE TEACHINGS OF A STOIC: SELECTED DISCOURSES AND THE ENCHIRIDION*, "HOW WE OUGHT TO USE DIVINATION" (FROM C. EARLY 2ND CENTURY CE)

COOPERATION WITH NATURE

What then is worth being valued? To be received with clapping of hands? No. Neither must we value the clapping of tongues, for the praise which comes from the many is a clapping of tongues. Suppose then that thou hast given up this worthless thing called fame, what remains that is worth valuing? This in my opinion, to move thyself and to restrain thyself in conformity to thy proper constitution, to which end both all employments and arts lead. For every art aims at this, that the thing which has been made should be adapted to the work for which it has been made; and both the vine-planter who looks after the vine, and the horse-breaker, and he who trains the dog, seek this end.

MARCUS AURELIUS, *MEDITATIONS*, "BOOK VI" (FROM C. 180 CE)

VIRTUE

Adorn thyself with simplicity and modesty and with indifference towards the things which lie between virtue and vice. Love mankind. Follow God. The poet says that Law rules all. And it is enough to remember that Law rules all.

MARCUS AURELIUS, *MEDITATIONS*, "BOOK VII" (FROM C. 180 CE)

WISDOM

Unexpected accidents are apt to strike deepest. Novelty adds weight to calamity, nor is there any mortal but who is more afflicted at what falls upon him by surprise. Nothing therefore should come upon us unexpectedly. The mind ought to be prepared not only against what usually happens but against whatever may happen. What is there that Fortune cannot throw down when she pleases from its most flourishing state?

LUCIUS SENECA, *LETTERS FROM A STOIC*, "XCI. OF NATURAL EVILS AND THE UNCERTAINTY OF HUMAN AFFAIRS" (FROM C. 63-65 CE)

COOPERATION WITH NATURE

…the universe consists of God and matter, that God rules and governs all things… Now, the Maker, i.e. God, must be greater than the things made, i.e., matter, which is ever subject to his Almighty power. And what God is in the world such is the mind or soul in man, what in the world is matter in us is body.

LUCIUS SENECA, *LETTERS FROM A STOIC*, "LXV. ON THE FIRST CAUSE" (FROM C. 63-65 CE)

VIRTUE

…modest actions preserve the modest man, and immodest actions destroy him; and actions of fidelity preserve the faithful man, and the contrary actions destroy him. And on the other hand contrary actions strengthen contrary characters: shamelessness strengthens the shameless man, faithlessness the faithless man, abusive words the abusive man, anger the man of an angry temper, and unequal receiving and giving make the avaricious man more avaricious. For this reason philosophers admonish us not to be satisfied with learning only, but also to add study, and then practice. For we have long been accustomed to do contrary things, and we put in practice opinions which are contrary to true opinions. If then we shall not also put in practice right opinions, we shall be nothing more than the expositors of the opinions of others.

EPICTETUS, *THE TEACHINGS OF A STOIC: SELECTED DISCOURSES AND THE ENCHIRIDION*, "THAT WHEN WE CANNOT FULFIL THAT WHICH THE CHARACTER OF A MAN PROMISES, WE ASSUME THE CHARACTER OF A PHILOSOPHER" (FROM C. EARLY 2ND CENTURY CE)

DETACHMENT

Wilt thou not cease to value many other things too? Then thou wilt be neither free, nor sufficient for thy own happiness, nor without passion. For of necessity thou must be envious, jealous, and suspicious of those who can take away those things, and plot against those who have that which is valued by thee. Of necessity a man must be altogether in a state of perturbation who wants any of these things; and besides, he must often find fault with the gods. But to reverence and honour thy own mind will make thee content with thyself, and in harmony with society, and in agreement with the gods, that is, praising all that they give and have ordered.

MARCUS AURELIUS, *MEDITATIONS*, "BOOK VI" (FROM C. 180 CE)

VIRTUE

Many praise thee, but are you satisfied with yourself if you are what they take you for and applaud? Let your goodness be approved within.

LUCIUS SENECA, *LETTERS FROM A STOIC*, "VII. ON PUBLIC SHOWS, PARTICULARLY THE GLADIATORS – AND CONVERSE WITH THE WORLD" (FROM C. 63-65 CE)

COOPERATION WITH NATURE

Consider who you are. In the first place, you are a man; and this is one who has nothing superior to the faculty of the will, but all other things subjected to it; and the faculty itself he possesses unenslaved and free from subjection. Consider then from what things you have been separated by reason. You have been separated from wild beasts; you have been separated from domestic animals. Further, you are a citizen of the world, and a part of it, not one of the subservient (serving), but one of the principal (ruling) parts, for you are capable of comprehending the divine administration and of considering the connection of things. What then does the character of a citizen promise (profess)? To hold nothing as profitable to himself; to deliberate about nothing as if he were detached from the community, but to act as the hand or foot would do, if they had reason and understood the constitution of nature, for they would never put themselves in motion nor desire anything otherwise than with reference to the whole.

EPICTETUS, *THE TEACHINGS OF A STOIC: SELECTED DISCOURSES AND THE ENCHIRIDION*, "HOW WE MAY DISCOVER THE DUTIES OF LIFE FROM NAMES" (FROM C. EARLY 2ND CENTURY CE)

NOBILITY OF THOUGHT

Every habit and faculty is maintained and increased by the corresponding actions: the habit of walking by walking, the habit of running by running. If you would be a good reader, read; if a writer, write. But when you shall not have read for thirty days in succession, but have done something else, you will know the consequence. In the same way, if you shall have lain down ten days, get up and attempt to make a long walk, and you will see how your legs are weakened. Generally then if you would make anything a habit, do it; if you would not make it a habit, do not do it, but accustom yourself to do something else in place of it. So it is with respect to the affections of the soul: when you have been angry, you must know that not only has this evil befallen you, but that you have also increased the habit, and in a manner thrown fuel upon fire.

EPICTETUS, *THE TEACHINGS OF A STOIC: SELECTED DISCOURSES AND THE ENCHIRIDION*, "HOW WE SHOULD STRUGGLE AGAINST APPEARANCES" (FROM C. EARLY 2ND CENTURY CE)

ACCEPTANCE

A man under present difficulties may comfort himself with saying, (Virgil) "an hour will come, with pleasure to relate Your sorrows past." But let him strive against them with all his might, he will certainly be overcome if he gives way, but if he bears up with patience and resolution against pain, he will overcome it.

LUCIUS SENECA, *LETTERS FROM A STOIC*, "LXXVIII. ON SICKNESS, PAIN AND DEATH" (FROM C. 63-65 CE)

VIRTUE

Indeed, we ought so to live as in the sight of man, and so to employ our thoughts as if the inmost recesses of our hearts were open to some inspector. They certainly are so, for what avails it to keep anything secret from man when we can hide nothing from God! He is intimate to our souls and interposeth himself in our common thoughts, so indeed as never absolutely to leave us.

LUCIUS SENECA, *LETTERS FROM A STOIC*, "LXXIX. ON DRUNKENNESS" (FROM C. 63-65 CE)

GOODNESS

Has then God given you eyes to no purpose? And to no purpose has he infused into them a spirit so strong and of such skilful contrivance as to reach a long way and to fashion the forms of things which are seen? What messenger is so swift and vigilant? … And to no purpose has he made light, without the presence of which there would be no use in any other thing? Man, be neither ungrateful for these gifts nor yet forget the things which are superior to them.

EPICTETUS, *THE TEACHINGS OF A STOIC: SELECTED DISCOURSES AND THE ENCHIRIDION*, "ON THE POWER OF SPEAKING" (FROM C. EARLY 2ND CENTURY CE)

NOBILITY OF THOUGHT

They are called liberal, you know, because they become a free man and are full worthy the application of a gentleman. But there is only one study or science that is truly liberal, viz. that which gives freedom indeed. And what is that but the study of wisdom, sublime, strong and manly?

LUCIUS SENECA, *LETTERS FROM A STOIC*, "LXXXVIII. ON LIBERAL SCIENCES" (FROM C. 63-65 CE)

WISDOM

The beginning of philosophy, to him at least who enters on it in the right way and by the door, is a consciousness of his own weakness and inability about necessary things; for we come into the world with no natural notion of a right-angled triangle, or of a diesis (a quarter tone), or of a half-tone; but we learn each of these things by a certain transmission according to art; and for this reason those who do not know them do not think that they know them. But as to good and evil, and beautiful and ugly, and becoming and unbecoming, and happiness and misfortune, and proper and improper, and what we ought to do and what we ought not to do, who ever came into the world without having an innate idea of them?

EPICTETUS, *THE TEACHINGS OF A STOIC: SELECTED DISCOURSES AND THE ENCHIRIDION*, "WHAT THE BEGINNING OF PHILOSOPHY IS" (FROM C. EARLY 2ND CENTURY CE)

VIRTUE

What do we admire? Externals. About what things are we busy? Externals. And have we any doubt then why we fear or why we are anxious? What then happens when we think the things, which are coming on us, to be evils? It is not in our power not to be afraid, it is not in our power not to be anxious. Then we say, Lord God, how shall I not be anxious? Fool, have you not hands, did not God make them for you? Sit down now and pray that your nose may not run. Wipe yourself rather and do not blame him. Well then, has he given to you nothing in the present case? Has he not given to you endurance? Has he not given to you magnanimity? Has he not given to you manliness? When you have such hands do you still look for one who shall wipe your nose?

EPICTETUS, *THE TEACHINGS OF A STOIC: SELECTED DISCOURSES AND THE ENCHIRIDION*, "THAT WE DO NOT STRIVE TO USE OUR OPINIONS ABOUT GOOD AND EVIL" (FROM C. EARLY 2ND CENTURY CE)

ACCEPTANCE

A journey cannot be said to be finished if you stop in the midway, or before you have reached the destined place, but the journey of life is such that it is at all times complete, provided it be just and honourable. Whenever you finish it, if finished well, it will be entire. Nay, it may sometimes be finished courageously even upon the slightest cause, for in truth there are no other that detain us here.

LUCIUS SENECA, *LETTERS FROM A STOIC*, "LXXVII. AGAINST THE FEAR OF DEATH" (FROM C. 63-65 CE)

NOBILITY OF THOUGHT

Take care that thou art not made into a Caesar, that thou art not dyed with this dye; for such things happen. Keep thyself then simple, good, pure, serious, free from affectation, a friend of justice, a worshipper of the gods, kind, affectionate, strenuous in all proper acts. Strive to continue to be such as philosophy wished to make thee. Reverence the gods, and help men. Short is life. There is only one fruit of this terrene life, a pious disposition and social acts.

MARCUS AURELIUS, *MEDITATIONS*, "BOOK VI" (FROM C. 180 CE)

DETACHMENT

…there is no profit from the things which are valued and eagerly sought to those who have obtained them; and to those who have not yet obtained them there is an imagination, that when these things are come, all that is good will come with them; then, when they are come, the feverish feeling is the same, the tossing to and fro is the same, the satiety, the desire of things, which are not present; for freedom is acquired not by the full possession of the things which are desired, but by removing the desire.

EPICTETUS, *THE TEACHINGS OF A STOIC: SELECTED DISCOURSES AND THE ENCHIRIDION*, "TO THOSE WHO FALL OFF (DESIST) FROM THEIR PURPOSE" (FROM C. EARLY 2ND CENTURY CE)

COOPERATION WITH NATURE

We have often reason to wish to die and yet we are
not willing, and when we really die, it is with regret.
No one indeed is so ignorant but that he knows he must die,
yet when the time draws near, he flinches, he trembles, he
weeps. Would you not think a man ridiculously foolish
who weeps because he did not live a thousand years ago?
It is equally absurd for him to weep because he shall not
live a thousand years hence. There is no difference between
"thou shalt not be" and "thou hast not been." In either of
these times you have no concern. Your lot is fallen upon
a point, which if you would prolong how many years
will you think to prolong it? Why do you weep?
What do you require? It is to no purpose.

LUCIUS SENECA, *LETTERS FROM A STOIC*, "LXXVII.
AGAINST THE FEAR OF DEATH" (FROM C. 63-65 CE)

WILL

If then I am there where my will is, then only shall I be a friend such as I ought to be, and son, and father; for this will be my interest, to maintain the character of fidelity, of modesty, of patience, of abstinence, of active cooperation, of observing my relations (towards all). But if I put myself in one place, and honesty in another, then the doctrine of Epicurus becomes strong, which asserts either that there is no honesty or it is that which opinion holds to be honest (virtuous).

EPICTETUS, *THE TEACHINGS OF A STOIC: SELECTED DISCOURSES AND THE ENCHIRIDION*, "ON FRIENDSHIP"
(FROM C. EARLY 2ND CENTURY CE)

ACCEPTANCE

Remember that in life you ought to behave as at a banquet. Suppose that something is carried round and is opposite to you. Stretch out your hand and take a portion with decency. Suppose that it passes by you. Do not detain it.

EPICTETUS, *THE TEACHINGS OF A STOIC: SELECTED DISCOURSES AND THE ENCHIRIDION*, "THE MANUAL: XV"
(FROM C. EARLY 2ND CENTURY CE)

COOPERATION WITH NATURE

Stop hoping you will change the will of the gods by praying. They are settled and fixed, they are conducted by a powerful and everlasting necessity. You will go where all things go. Is there anything strange in this? You were born upon these conditions: your parents, your ancestors and all posterity are subject to the same. A chain of causes, invincible and invariable, binds and draws all things with it. What numbers shall follow you when you are dead! How many shall accompany you in death! I am persuaded that you would be more contagious if thousands were to die with you. Know then that, at this very moment in which you make such a difficulty in dying, thousands of men and other animals are breathing their last by various kinds of death. And did you not think you should one day reach the place to which you have been travelling your whole life? Every journey has its end.

LUCIUS SENECA, *LETTERS FROM A STOIC*, "LXXVII. AGAINST THE FEAR OF DEATH" (FROM C. 63-65 CE)

VIRTUE

Grammarian's principal study is to speak accurately, and if he launcheth out any further it is to have some knowledge in history… Now what is therein all these that leads to virtue? The weighing of syllables and the propriety of words, the remembrance of stories, the scanning of verses and the laws of poetry? Which of these can take away fear, can root out a fond desire, or bridle headstrong lust? Let us pass on to geometry and, if you please, to music; you will find nothing in either of them that forbids fear or restrains desire, which passions, unless a man knows how to govern, all other knowledge is but vain. Let us consider whether the professors of the forementioned qualifications teach virtue or not, if they do not teach it they transmit it not, if they do teach it, they are more than what they profess themselves to be, they are philosophers. Would you know how little they are concerned in teaching virtue, only observe what a difference there is in their several studies. But their studies would be alike if they taught the same thing…

LUCIUS SENECA, *LETTERS FROM A STOIC*, "LXXXVIII. ON LIBERAL SCIENCES" (FROM C. 63-65 CE)

VIRTUE

339

For when you have once desired money, if reason be applied to lead to a perception of the evil, the desire is stopped, and the ruling faculty of our mind is restored to the original authority. But if you apply no means of cure, it no longer returns to the same state, but being again excited by the corresponding appearance, it is inflamed to desire quicker than before: and when this takes place continually, it is henceforth hardened (made callous), and the disease of the mind confirms the love of money.

EPICTETUS, *THE TEACHINGS OF A STOIC: SELECTED DISCOURSES AND THE ENCHIRIDION*, "HOW WE SHOULD STRUGGLE AGAINST APPEARANCES" (FROM C. EARLY 2ND CENTURY CE)

TIME

340

Death, my friend, ought to be placed before the eyes of the young as well as of the old. For we are not summoned according to the parish register. And besides, there is no man so old as to make it sinful to expect another day. Now every day is another step in life.

LUCIUS SENECA, *LETTERS FROM A STOIC*, "XII. ON LIFE AND OLD AGE" (FROM C. 63-65 CE)

VIRTUE

One thing here is worth a great deal, to pass thy life in truth and justice, with a benevolent disposition even to liars and unjust men. When thou wishest to delight thyself, think of the virtues of those who live with thee; for instance, the activity of one, and the modesty of another, and the liberality of a third, and some other good quality of a fourth.

MARCUS AURELIUS, *MEDITATIONS*, "BOOK VI" (FROM C. 180 CE)

GOODNESS

My friends indeed contributed somewhat thereto, having supported and comforted me with their good counsel, watchings and discourses. Nothing, my Lucilius, best of men, so revives and helps a man in sickness as the affectionate tenders of a friend. Nothing so much alleviates and steals away the expectation and fear of death. So long as these should live I did not think I could die. I thought, I say, I should still live if not in their company yet in their memory, and that I was not pouring out my spirit but delivering it up to them.

LUCIUS SENECA, *LETTERS FROM A STOIC*, "LXXVIII. ON SICKNESS, PAIN AND DEATH" (FROM C. 63-65 CE)

GOODNESS

[Nature] showeth us what is truly evil and what only seems so, she roots out vanity from the mind and implanteth solid greatness. She next enquires into the nature of the soul, from whence it was derived, examining the truth and all the arguments relating thereto.

LUCIUS SENECA, *LETTERS FROM A STOIC*, "XC. ON PHILOSOPHY AND THE INVENTION OF ARTS" (FROM C. 63-65 CE)

VIRTUE

On the occasion of every accident (event) that befalls you, remember to turn to yourself and inquire what power you have for turning it to use. If you see a fair man or a fair woman, you will find that the power to resist is temperance (continence). If labour (pain) be presented to you, you will find that it is endurance. If it be abusive words, you will find it to be patience. And if you have been thus formed to the (proper) habit, the appearances will not carry you along with them.

EPICTETUS, *THE TEACHINGS OF A STOIC: SELECTED DISCOURSES AND THE ENCHIRIDION*, "THE MANUAL: X" (FROM C. EARLY 2ND CENTURY CE)

NOBILITY OF THOUGHT

Make not therefore thine afflictions more grievous than they are by impatience and heavy complaints, the pain is light when not aggravated by fancy and opinion. If you can be persuaded to comfort yourself with saying, "it is nothing, or in effect very little, let us bear it patiently," it will be soon at an end, or this very thought will make it easy and tolerable. All things depend upon opinion, not only ambition but even luxury and avarice refer to it. Pain also is proportioned to opinion. Everyone is as wretched as he thinks himself to be.

LUCIUS SENECA, *LETTERS FROM A STOIC*, "LXXVIII. ON SICKNESS, PAIN AND DEATH" (FROM C. 63-65 CE)

WILL

He who loves fame considers another man's activity to be his own good; and he who loves pleasure, his own sensations; but he who has understanding, considers his own acts to be his own good. It is in our power to have no opinion about a thing, and not to be disturbed in our soul; for things themselves have no natural power to form our judgements… No man will hinder thee from living according to the reason of thy own nature: nothing will happen to thee contrary to the reason of the universal nature.

MARCUS AURELIUS, *MEDITATIONS*, "BOOK VI" (FROM C. 180 CE)

GOODNESS

I could name several who wanted not a friend but friendship. Now this cannot happen where minds are possessed with a uniformity of will to act honourably. And why can it not? Because they know that all things, and more especially adversity, are to be held in common.

LUCIUS SENECA, *LETTERS FROM A STOIC*, "VI. ON FRIENDSHIP AND CONVERSATION" (FROM C. 63-65 CE)

NOBILITY OF THOUGHT

To whom then does the contemplation of these matters (philosophical inquiries) belong? To him who has leisure, for man is an animal that loves contemplation.

EPICTETUS, *THE TEACHINGS OF A STOIC: SELECTED DISCOURSES AND THE ENCHIRIDION*, "ON CONSTANCY (OR FIRMNESS)" (FROM C. EARLY 2ND CENTURY CE)

TIME

What avails it to reflect upon the pains we have suffered and to make ourselves miserable because we were once so? Besides, there is no one but who makes some additions to his misfortunes and often gives himself the lie. Not but that there is a certain pleasure in recounting past sufferings, and it is natural to rejoice in an escape. There are two things therefore to be particularly renounced: "the fear of what may happen and the recollection of an evil past." The one is no concern to me now, nor need I anticipate the other.

LUCIUS SENECA, *LETTERS FROM A STOIC*, "LXXVIII. ON SICKNESS, PAIN AND DEATH" (FROM C. 63-65 CE)

DETACHMENT

When you see a person weeping in sorrow either when a child goes abroad or when he is dead, or when the man has lost his property, take care that the appearance do not hurry you away with it, as if he were suffering in external things. But straightway make a distinction in your own mind, and be in readiness to say, it is not that which has happened that afflicts this man, for it does not afflict another, but it is the opinion about this thing which afflicts the man. So far as words then do not be unwilling to show him sympathy, and even if it happens so, to lament with him. But take care that you do not lament internally also.

EPICTETUS, *THE TEACHINGS OF A STOIC: SELECTED DISCOURSES AND THE ENCHIRIDION*, "THE MANUAL: XVI" (FROM C. EARLY 2ND CENTURY CE)

TIME

If any god told thee that thou shalt die tomorrow, or certainly on the day after tomorrow, thou wouldst not care much whether it was on the third day or on the morrow, unless thou wast in the highest degree mean-spirited – for how small is the difference? So think it no great thing to die after as many years as thou canst name rather than tomorrow.

MARCUS AURELIUS, *MEDITATIONS*, "BOOK IV"
(FROM C. 180 CE)

DETACHMENT

Thus, how great part so ever of things, or human or divine, you at present comprehend you will still find matter enough to employ and fatigue the mind in the search of farther truths. That things therefore so many and of so great consequence may find place for their reception, it is necessary that all that are superfluous should be removed from the mind.

LUCIUS SENECA, *LETTERS FROM A STOIC*, "LXXXVIII.
ON LIBERAL SCIENCES" (FROM C. 63-65 CE)

CHANGE

For he who has had a fever, and has been relieved from it, is not in the same state that he was before, unless he has been completely cured. Something of the kind happens also in diseases of the soul. Certain traces and blisters are left in it, and unless a man shall completely efface them, when he is again lashed on the same places, the lash will produce not blisters (weals) but sores. If then you wish not to be of an angry temper, do not feed the habit: throw nothing on it which will increase it: at first keep quiet, and count the days on which you have not been angry. I used to be in passion every day; now every second day; then every third, then every fourth. But if you have intermitted thirty days, make a sacrifice to God. For the habit at first begins to be weakened, and then is completely destroyed… Be willing at length to be approved by yourself, be willing to appear beautiful to God, desire to be in purity with your own pure self and with God.

EPICTETUS, *THE TEACHINGS OF A STOIC: SELECTED DISCOURSES AND THE ENCHIRIDION*, "HOW WE SHOULD STRUGGLE AGAINST APPEARANCES" (FROM C. EARLY 2ND CENTURY CE)

DETACHMENT

Things themselves (materials) are indifferent; but the use of them is not indifferent. How then shall a man preserve firmness and tranquillity, and at the same time be careful and neither rash nor negligent? If he imitates those who play at dice. The counters are indifferent; the dice are indifferent. How do I know what the cast will be? But to use carefully and dexterously the cast of the dice, this is my business. Thus then in life also the chief business is this: distinguish and separate things, and say: Externals are not in my power: will is in my power. Where shall I seek the good and the bad? Within, in the things which are my own. But in what does not belong to you call nothing either good or bad, or profit or damage or anything of the kind.

EPICTETUS, *THE TEACHINGS OF A STOIC: SELECTED DISCOURSES AND THE ENCHIRIDION*, "HOW MAGNANIMITY IS CONSISTENT WITH CARE" (FROM C. EARLY 2ND CENTURY CE)

TIME

What then, know you not, that it is one of the duties of life, to die? You forego no duty, for the number of them being uncertain, what was incumbent upon you is already finished. There is no life that can be called long.

LUCIUS SENECA, *LETTERS FROM A STOIC*, "LXXVII. AGAINST THE FEAR OF DEATH" (FROM C. 63-65 CE)

WILL

…if you would prove that a good man ought never to be drunk, what need is there of having recourse to syllogism? Rather show how ridiculous and vile a thing it is for a man to pour down more than he can hold and not to know the strength of his constitution. How many things drunken men are apt to do which when sober they would be ashamed of. And that drunkenness is nothing else but a voluntary madness. And suppose this evil habit to grow upon a man, can you doubt of its being somewhat more than madness, even rage and fury? The fit is not less though it be shorter.

LUCIUS SENECA, *LETTERS FROM A STOIC*, "LXXIX. ON DRUNKENNESS" (FROM C. 63-65 CE)

COOPERATION WITH NATURE

Dost thou not see the little plants, the little birds, the ants, the spiders, the bees working together to put in order their several parts of the universe? And art thou unwilling to do the work of a human being, and dost thou not make haste to do that which is according to thy nature? But it is necessary to take rest also. It is necessary: however nature has fixed bounds to this too: she has fixed bounds both to eating and drinking, and yet thou goest beyond these bounds, beyond what is sufficient; yet in thy acts it is not so, but thou stoppest short of what thou canst do. So thou lovest not thyself, for if thou didst, thou wouldst love thy nature and her will.

MARCUS AURELIUS, *MEDITATIONS*, "BOOK V" (FROM C. 180 CE)

NOBILITY OF THOUGHT

How much trouble he avoids who does not look to see what his neighbour says or does or thinks, but only to what he does himself, that it may be just and pure; or as Agathon says, look not round at the depraved morals of others, but run straight along the line without deviating from it.

MARCUS AURELIUS, *MEDITATIONS*, "BOOK IV" (FROM C. 180 CE)

WILL

Thus we also act: in what cases do we fear? In things which are independent of the will. In what cases on the contrary do we behave with confidence, as if there were no danger? In things dependent on the will. To be deceived then, or to act rashly, or shamelessly, or with base desire to seek something, does not concern us at all, if we only hit the mark in things which are independent of our will. But where there is death or exile or pain or infamy, there we attempt to run away, there we are struck with terror. Therefore, as we may expect it to happen with those who err in the greatest matters, we convert natural confidence (that is, according to nature) into audacity, desperation, rashness, shamelessness; and we convert natural caution and modesty into cowardice and meanness, which are full of fear and confusion.

EPICTETUS, *THE TEACHINGS OF A STOIC: SELECTED DISCOURSES AND THE ENCHIRIDION*, "THAT CONFIDENCE (COURAGE) IS NOT INCONSISTENT WITH CAUTION" (FROM C. EARLY 2ND CENTURY CE)

ACCEPTANCE

But we shall easily endure these things, weak broths, warm water and whatever the delicate and luxurious, and such as are rather sick in mind than in body think intolerable, if we once get over the horror and fear of death. And this we certainly shall do if we rightly distinguished the ends of good and evil, for by this means neither life would seem tedious or distasteful nor death terrible.

LUCIUS SENECA, *LETTERS FROM A STOIC*, "LXXVIII. ON SICKNESS, PAIN AND DEATH" (FROM C. 63-65 CE)

GOODNESS

The perfection of moral character consists in this, in passing every day as the last, and in being neither violently excited nor torpid nor playing the hypocrite… But thou, who art destined to end so soon, art thou wearied of enduring the bad, and this too when thou art one of them? It is a ridiculous thing for a man not to fly from his own badness, which is indeed possible, but to fly from other men's badness, which is impossible.

MARCUS AURELIUS, *MEDITATIONS*, "BOOK VII" (FROM C. 180 CE)

DETACHMENT

…we ought not to desire in every way what is not our own. And the sorrow of another is another's sorrow; but my sorrow is my own. I then will stop my own sorrow by every means, for it is in my power; and the sorrow of another I will endeavour to stop as far as I can; but I will not attempt to do it by every means; for if I do, I shall be fighting against God…

EPICTETUS, *THE TEACHINGS OF A STOIC: SELECTED DISCOURSES AND THE ENCHIRIDION*, "THE MANUAL: L" (FROM C. EARLY 2ND CENTURY CE)

VIRTUE

Remember that it is not he who reviles you or strikes you, who insults you, but it is your opinion about these things as being insulting. When then a man irritates you, you must know that it is your own opinion which has irritated you.

EPICTETUS, *THE TEACHINGS OF A STOIC: SELECTED DISCOURSES AND THE ENCHIRIDION*, "THE MANUAL: XX" (FROM C. EARLY 2ND CENTURY CE)

WISDOM

I dissent from those who defy a storm, and not disliking a public and busy life are continually exerting their courage in struggling with and getting through difficulties. A wise man would endure this if it fell to his lot, but he would by no means make it his choice. ... For it is of little avail to him to have thrown off his own vices if he must be perpetually contending with those of other men.

LUCIUS SENECA, *LETTERS FROM A STOIC*, "XXVIII. CHANGE OF PLACE MAKES NO ALTERATION IN THE MIND" (FROM C. 63-65 CE)

WILL

[Sickness] fetters the feet of the running-footman and will tie up the hands of the cobbler and blacksmith, but if you have learned the right use of the mind you will still give advice, teach, hear, learn, be inquisitive, reflect and the like. Besides, do you think you are doing nothing if you are temperate in your sickness? You will hereby show that your distemper may be conquered or at least supported with patience.

LUCIUS SENECA, *LETTERS FROM A STOIC*, "LXXVIII. ON SICKNESS, PAIN AND DEATH" (FROM C. 63-65 CE)

INDEX BY THEME

ACCEPTANCE

16, 24, 25, 34, 44, 52, 53, 64, 65, 66, 70, 74, 81, 101, 103, 108, 117, 118, 140, 146, 150, 160, 169, 183, 187, 197, 224, 228, 231, 247

CHANGE

38, 51, 57, 61, 72, 79, 89, 93, 100, 102, 112, 115, 118, 120, 121, 129, 136, 141, 142, 143, 152, 156, 157, 164, 182, 190, 210, 215, 242

COOPERATION WITH NATURE

20, 23, 28, 30, 31, 46, 49, 57, 69, 81, 94, 96, 97, 109, 119, 130, 139, 147, 148, 151, 152, 155, 156, 158, 164, 178, 183, 184, 188, 192, 199, 206, 207, 209, 214, 218, 219, 222, 230, 232, 245

DETACHMENT

17, 18, 25, 35, 39, 43, 50, 65, 71, 73, 76, 85, 86, 87, 88, 107, 109, 110, 113, 114, 117, 121, 124, 130, 132, 133, 134, 149, 155, 161, 166, 168, 171, 175, 179, 180, 182, 185, 188, 189, 192, 197, 203, 204, 206, 207, 212, 221, 229, 240, 241, 243, 248

GOODNESS

19, 23, 44, 56, 60, 62, 68, 75, 83, 87, 89, 107, 114, 115, 122, 123, 125, 135, 137, 138, 144, 159, 162, 168, 176, 199, 201, 225, 235, 236, 238, 247

NOBILITY OF THOUGHT

26, 31, 45, 47, 55, 59, 63, 72, 80, 90, 92, 100, 105, 113, 122, 142, 145, 153, 158, 165, 170, 172, 173, 174, 179, 181, 186, 196, 198, 203, 216, 223, 225, 228, 237, 239, 245

TIME

17, 35, 36, 42, 48, 53, 61, 64, 74, 76, 77, 79, 84, 92, 128, 149, 151, 169, 174, 189, 234, 239, 241, 244

VIRTUE

15, 16, 20, 21, 22, 33, 37, 39, 40, 41, 42, 43, 50, 51, 54, 58, 59, 60, 67, 73, 75, 78, 80, 95, 106, 125, 127, 129, 134, 136, 141, 143, 153, 167, 191, 193, 194, 201, 205, 208, 213, 217, 218, 220, 221, 224, 227, 233, 234, 235, 236, 248

WILL

28, 29, 34, 36, 40, 48, 83, 86, 91, 95, 97, 98, 108, 126, 131, 137, 172, 175, 195, 200, 231, 238, 244, 246, 249

WISDOM

19, 22, 24, 27, 29, 30, 32, 33, 37, 41, 52, 54, 63, 67, 68, 82, 84, 99, 101, 102, 104, 105, 111, 112, 116, 133, 147, 154, 163, 177, 185, 202, 210, 211, 213, 219, 226, 249

INDEX BY STOIC

AMBROSE, ST
11

ANTIPATER OF TARSUS
11

ARRIAN
11, 13

AUGUSTINE, ST
11

BECK, AARON T.
12

BOETHIUS
11

CATO THE YOUNGER
11

CHRYSIPPUS
11

CLEANTHES
11

CRATES OF THEBES
10–11

DESCARTES, RENÉ
11

DIOGENES OF BABYLON
11

ELLIS, ALBERT
12

EPICTETUS
11, 13, 15, 17, 18, 21, 22, 23, 25, 27, 33, 34, 35, 36, 40, 41, 44, 48, 49, 52, 56, 59, 62, 64, 65, 66, 70, 73, 76, 78, 81, 84, 86, 89, 91, 92, 95, 96, 97, 99, 102, 105, 107, 109, 110, 112, 113, 114, 116, 117, 119, 121, 122, 126, 130, 132, 133, 134, 135, 140, 141, 142, 143, 145, 149, 150, 151, 153, 161, 163,

164, 166, 169, 170, 172, 176, 178, 180, 182, 184, 185, 187, 188, 189, 190, 192, 198, 200, 201, 202, 203, 204, 205, 206, 207, 209, 214, 217, 220, 222, 223, 225, 226, 227, 229, 231, 234, 236, 239, 240, 242, 243, 246, 248

JEROME, ST
11

JUSTUS LÍPSIUS
11

MARCUS AURELIUS ANTONINUS
6–8, 11, 13–14, 16, 17, 20, 24, 25, 29, 30, 31, 35, 37, 38, 40, 42, 43, 44, 46, 47, 48, 51, 53, 54, 55, 57, 60, 61, 63, 64, 69, 71, 73, 74, 75, 76, 79, 81, 83, 84, 86, 88, 89, 92, 94, 95, 97, 98, 100, 101, 104, 105, 107, 109, 112, 115, 122, 125, 128, 130, 131, 134, 136, 137, 138, 139, 141, 146, 151, 152, 153, 155, 156, 158, 159, 164, 168, 169, 171, 174, 179, 182, 183, 185, 188, 189, 192, 194, 197, 199, 206, 210, 213, 215, 218, 221, 228, 235, 238, 241, 245, 247

MUSONIUS RUFUS
13

PANAETIUS OF RHODES
11

PASCAL, BLAISE
11

SENECA, LUCIUS ANNAEUS
8, 11, 12, 16, 19, 22, 23, 24, 26, 28, 29, 30, 31, 32, 36, 37, 39, 42, 45, 50, 54, 58, 59, 60, 63, 67, 68, 72, 74, 75, 77, 79, 80, 82, 83, 85, 87, 90, 93, 100, 102, 103, 106, 108, 111, 113, 114, 115, 117, 118, 120, 121, 123, 124, 125, 127, 128, 129, 133, 136, 138, 139, 142, 144, 147, 149, 148, 152, 154, 157, 158, 160, 162, 165, 167, 168, 173, 174, 175, 177, 181, 183, 186, 191, 193, 195, 196, 197, 201, 207, 208, 211, 212, 213, 216, 219, 221, 224, 225, 228, 230, 232, 233, 234, 235, 236, 237, 238, 239, 241, 244, 247, 249

SPINOZA, BENEDICT
11

ZENO OF CITIUM
10–11

ZENO OF TARSUS
11

FURTHER READING

All the quotes in this book were sourced from the following original texts:

Meditations, Marcus Aurelius
(Collins Classics, 2020)

Letters from a Stoic, Lucius Seneca
(Collins Classics, 2025)

The Teachings of a Stoic: Selected Discourses and the Encheiridion, Epictetus
(Collins Classics, 2023)

ACKNOWLEDGEMENTS

When I was asked to create this little book I nearly jumped out of my skin with non-Stoical exuberance. This project gave me the excuse to spend a significant amount of my time with three very fine minds who perplexed and challenged me for weeks on end. As I predicted (and hoped), this book project became the most cathartic one I have taken on thus far, and I honestly don't know how I got through life before absorbing this perennial Stoic wisdom.

A hearty thanks to my ever-encouraging, resilient and enthusiastic editor, Simon Holland, who made a very tight deadline seem more like a fun challenge than a headache!